LENTEN

POSTCARDS

DAILY DEVOTIONS

INSPIRED BY

The BOOK *of*

Common Prayer

f▸

THE FOUNDRY
PUBLISHING

CONTENTS

INTRODUCTION

The season of Lent is altogether at home in the Wesleyan-Holiness tradition. While it has not been as prominent a feature in evangelicalism in generations past, the season of Lent bears the emphases that are so much at the heart of evangelicalism: an awareness of our need for grace, a deep conviction of sin, a profound appreciation for the sufferings of Christ on our behalf, and a hunger to be shaped and formed into greater likeness to Jesus.

In the early church, the season of Lent was typically the time during which new believers were prepared for their anticipated baptism into the Christian faith. That initiatory rite often occurred on Easter Sunday. The season was therefore focused on spiritual preparation, repentance, and the forming of new habits and new relationships, accompanied by fasting, catechetical instruction, and spiritual guidance.

Through intentional engagement of this unique season, we are reconnected to our human frailty and to our continual need to turn to Jesus for healing, hope, and holiness. Our eyes do not stay fixed on our sin, failure, or mortality but are drawn with an ever-increasing intensity to the Savior. The Lenten season—leading us toward the celebration of Easter with awe, gratitude, and humility—guides us through a time of needed introspection, of confession of our need for the grace revealed at Calvary. It is a good season for a renewal of spiritual disciplines like fasting, acts of compassion, self-examination, and guided reading of Scripture.

As can be the case in any repeated spiritual endeavor, when the purposes for which the season is intended are blurred by familiarity, lack of personal engagement, and mere form, the season loses its intensity and effectiveness. But familiarity need not breed contempt. Faithful, disciplined observance of the Lenten season can be a conduit of authentic transformation and discipleship. Lives are changed, destinies are altered, cultures are impacted, and the church can grow in depth and breadth.

The season of Lent begins on Ash Wednesday and ends on Holy Saturday before Easter. The date is set by the same cycle that determines the date for Easter. Lent is traditionally understood as the forty weekdays during the season leading up to Easter Sunday. The Sundays in Lent are intended to be focused on worship and adoration and are thereby not technically considered part of the Lenten season. On Sundays in Lent, the fasts or other self-denial exercises are set aside, to be resumed on the Monday following.

The resources for following the Lenten tradition are varied. The *Book of Common Prayer* provides recommended daily Scripture readings and Sunday readings based on a two-year cycle. The Revised Common Lectionary, which operates on a three-year cycle, provides alternate weekly Scripture readings for the Sundays in the Lenten season.

In this devotional guide the Scripture readings are for Year Two, as indicated for the year 2020 in the *Book of Common Prayer*. The devotionals will focus much of their attention on the Gospel reading for each day, drawing insight also from the various other Scripture recommendations for the day. The devotionals for each Sunday during Lent will also draw from the *Book of Common Prayer* schedule. Churches that utilize the Revised Common Lectionary will have the option of using either resource for Sundays during Lent.

It is our prayer that this Lenten journey will provide you with spiritual guidance as you participate in this sacred season. May Christ himself draw near to you as you open yourself to the probing of the Holy Spirit and the Word of God. Examine your heart, open your mind to new insight, and prepare yourself to celebrate the resurrection on Easter Sunday with joy and gratitude.

Jesse C Middendorf
Stephanie Dyrness Lobdell

ASH WEDNESDAY

AM *Psalms: 95, 32, 143*

PM *Psalms: 102, 130*

Amos 5:6–15

Luke 18:9–14

Hebrews 12:1–14

We were only months into our very first pastoral assignment when, as a result of a habit I had quickly formed, I was reading the newspaper during our morning breakfast. Suddenly and without warning, the newspaper exploded from my hands and fell to the floor. I found myself staring into the blazing eyes of my beautiful wife. "*TALK* to me!" she said, with emphasis.

After my first startled reaction, I began to realize that in my zeal to stay informed, be relevant in my preaching and leadership, and in my desire to see what people were saying and thinking and doing in the world around us, I was neglecting to communicate with the one person most important to me in my life. Fifty-five years later, I still recall those piercing eyes.

"Seek the LORD," said Amos to Israel. "You are preoccupied with your own agendas, running here and there in your vain attempts at worship, and still withholding justice from the poor, lying to preserve your advantage over others, and ignoring the cries of God trying to get your attention."

There is certainly enough noise to hold our attention in this world. The urgent voices of newscasters, the angry accusations and recriminations of politicians and government leaders, contentious cultural relationships, and even the tensions at work in many of our churches—all make a claim on our emotions, our attention, and our spiritual well-being. Much like the Pharisee in the parable Jesus told in Luke 18, it is an easy step into utter blindness in our spiritual journey.

Lent is our wake-up call. This is a season for serious and sustained attention to our need for honest self-examination, piercing honesty with God, and humble contrition. It is a risky step to read Psalm 51 and assure ourselves that we are not like King David. While we may have avoided the devastation of a public moral failure, we must not miss the painful reality that our world would be much different if followers of Jesus Christ were actually more like Jesus. If we were focused less on our own personal preferences, our self-absorption, and our easy criticism of those not like us, we might find ourselves on our faces, acknowledging our own spiritual emptiness. This is the Lenten journey.

In this season, we are invited to face our mortality, and it is a mercy. This reminder is the gift of Lent. We are reminded that we are powerless to save ourselves. This realization moves us to repentance as we acknowledge our desperate need for a Savior, and to worship as we are reminded of God's provision for us in Jesus. As we take this forty-six-day journey with Jesus toward the cross, let's embrace our own mortality. Let's humbly acknowledge that the sufferings of Christ were for us. And let's heed the gracious invitation of Lent to enter into an intimate encounter with Jesus on this journey toward Jerusalem. He is trying to get your attention. Are you listening?

—JCM

REFLECTION & PRACTICE

01 As you begin this Lenten journey, do an honest inventory of your life. In what ways might you be preoccupied with your own agenda and missing what God wants to do in and through you?

02 As in the Amos passage, preoccupation with our own agendas can lead us to self-serving habits that ultimately do damage to the weak among us. In a similar way, David's preoccupation with his own desires led to the abusive treatment of Bathsheba and murder of her husband. In what ways might unhealthy, self-centered patterns in your life be hurting those around you?

03 Lent is a season in which we set aside good things (or morally neutral things) to make space for better things. Do you find yourself turning to specific habits for comfort or affirmation? What might it look like to set aside those habits and allow yourself to feel your need for Christ?

04 In addition to setting aside certain habits, we are encouraged to take up new habits that draw our attention off ourselves and fix it on Jesus. Works of mercy and practical expressions of compassion and justice help us direct energy that was formerly devoted to pursuing our own agendas into serving others. How might you intentionally seek out opportunities to embody compassion and justice this Lenten season?

PRAYER

Lord, as we journey to the cross with you this Lenten season, we confess that we are often consumed by our own agendas. We fail to love you with our whole hearts and others as ourselves. We acknowledge our inability to save ourselves and invite you once again to reorient us rightly. We repent of our self-serving habits and give your Spirit full permission to convict us of any patterns or practices that are drawing our hearts away from you. Open our eyes to ways we might serve others selflessly in compassion and justice for the sake of your coming kingdom. Thank you for making a way for us through your Son, and thank you for giving us the gift of your Spirit, who empowers us to obey.

THURSDAY

AM *Psalm: 37:1–18*

PM *Psalm: 37:19–40*

Habakkuk 3:1–18

John 17:1–8

Philippians 3:12–21

"Father, the hour has come."

One of the stunning purposes behind the tradition of Ash Wednesday is to remind us of our own mortality. With the imposition of ashes—the ancient symbol of mourning—we are faced with the fact that, if the Lord tarries, our lives as we know them will end. One response to that reminder is resignation: "Well, we all have to go sometime."

Today's Gospel reading recalls an altogether different way of facing our going. Jesus has just poured his heart into the disciples in the upper room. His final words to them were pointed. In John 16:32, he told them they would desert him. Then he turned his eyes toward heaven and began to speak to the Father: "The hour has come." This was anything but resignation. Jesus was on the verge of everything for which he had existed in human form since his conception. This was fulfillment. This was to be his enthronement, his lifting up by which he would draw all humanity to himself. "Glorify your Son . . ."

But we must be careful not to read into the prayer of Jesus a mere dismissal of what he was to face. Though he was divine, he was also utterly, completely human. His agony in the garden of Gethsemane was not theater. It was fear and uncertainty, with a fervent and altogether human plea for deliverance from what was ahead. This was Satan, returning, attempting to face Jesus down, just as he had promised he would do. Yet, as events unfolded on that tumultuous evening, Jesus could say, "Father, the hour has come."

Another response to our own mortality is fear and uncertainty, aptly demonstrated in the experience of Simon Peter following the arrest of Jesus. His bold assertions of loyalty and courage melted in the face of a young girl's pointing finger. He had, like all the other disciples, turned away in terror as Jesus was apprehended. Though Peter was desperate to see what was happening to Jesus in the courtyard of the high priest, when the confrontation came to him personally, fear won the moment, and Peter cursed and denied knowing or being associated with Jesus.

This Lenten journey should bring us to our knees in recognition that, apart from the power and presence of the Holy Spirit, we are powerless to stare down our own fear of death. However, the prayer of Jesus should give us hope. Death is not the foe it thinks it is. The Father did indeed glorify the Son—and he will give us glory!

—JCM

REFLECTION & PRACTICE

01 We live in a culture that idolizes life and avoids death, delaying it at almost any cost. How do the death and resurrection of Jesus invite us to surrender our fear and attempts at control?

02 Embracing our mortality is not resignation or surrender but a confession of our inability to save ourselves and order the world rightly. Reflect on the ways in which your life might become a confession of Christ's lordship, even unto death.

03 Even as we accept the limits of our mortality and acknowledge God as the source of salvation and redemption, we recognize that we are

invited to partner with God in the work of redemption in this life. How might you partner with God in the work of redemption, and labor for the good of the world as an act of obedient trust in the coming reign of God?

PRAYER

Lord, thank you for the gift of our mortality. We confess we have not always received it as such and have strained against the gift, bound as we are by the illusion of our own lordship. Awaken our hearts to our mortality and enable us to receive it well in full trust that what you did in Jesus, you will do in us, resurrecting and redeeming us, to order us rightly. May we find peace in the knowledge that you are the source of the redemption of all creation even as we partner with you in that holy work.

FRIDAY

AM *Psalms: 95, 31*

PM *Psalm: 35*

Ezekiel 18:1–4, 25–32

John 17:9–19

Philippians 4:1–9

The Lenten journey is intended to lead us toward the cross where Jesus was crucified. We are invited to join this journey with a deepening sense of the tragedy that begins to unfold before us. It is also a journey of introspection. We consciously are confronted by our own need to take a new look at why Jesus was crucified.

A student asked a New Testament professor an oft-repeated question: "If I were the only person on earth, would Jesus have died for me?"

The professor's immediate response was, "If you were the only person on earth, *you* would have crucified Jesus!"

In the Gospel reading for today, Jesus prays to the Father for his disciples. He is certain the disciples will face significant challenges if they choose to continue to follow him as those who will represent all that Jesus said and did while he lived. He implores the Father to protect them. "The world has hated them," he says, "for they are not of the world."

Jesus knows they will face temptation, opposition, assault, indifference. "Protect them," he says.

It is no secret that following Jesus is a daunting task. The pressure on anyone who chooses to follow Jesus passionately will be intense. And much of the pressure will come not so much from others as it will from our own frailty, our own humanity. Many of us prefer to live our lives in quiet, private devotion rather than public, conspicuous discipleship. We prefer confession of our frailty in our closets to transparent, honest vulnerability. Our resistance to vulnerability hinders our ability to engage in Christian community faithfully because we are bound up in pride and fear.

Writing to the Philippian church, Paul pleads with two women with whom he worked closely in service to the gospel. "Help them get along," he urges his friend. Often it is not the opponents of the gospel who are our greatest obstacle. It is the people with whom we work the closest. And the problem is not so much them as it is us. This is where the evil one does the most damage to our journey. It is so hard to see our own culpability in places where we are in tension with other believers. That is why the psalmist would say, "He is our God, and we are the people of his pasture, the flock under his care," and in the next sentence cries out, "Today, if only you would hear his voice . . ." (95:7).

That is why a discerning professor would say, "If you were the only person on earth, you would have crucified Jesus!"

It is hard for us to embrace the cross. The cross forces us to acknowledge our complicity with the powers of sin and death.

Oh, God! Please answer the prayer of Jesus. Sanctify us!

—JCM

REFLECTION & PRACTICE

01 Participation in the in-breaking kingdom of God is impossible apart from the recognition of and repentance from our complicity in the brokenness of creation. What role might Christian community play in our confession and restoration?

02 In today's Gospel passage, Jesus expresses the desire that his followers be one as he and the Father are one. The relationship between Jesus and the Father is one marked by humble trust, self-giving love,

and a shared mission. How might that divine relationship shape how we interact with fellow disciples?

03 It is easy to be unified with those who look and think like we do. Christian unity, however, is based not on mutual affinity, parallel political positions, or theological conformity but, rather, on a shared commitment to obedience to Jesus and his way. How might you intentionally seek out relationship with disciples who differ from you in significant ways? How might God be honored in our mutual submission and cooperative service?

PRAYER

Lord, we humbly confess our complicity in the brokenness in and around us. Often, we ignore your call to unity and instead surround ourselves with others who think, look, and act like us. We choose postures of pride and self-righteousness instead of humble vulnerability. We recognize that, apart from your sanctifying work in us, we are powerless to free ourselves from the bondage of our sin. Free us from ourselves and make us, your body, one in you. Protect us from the siren call of secularism that deafens us to your correcting and comforting voice. May our life together serve as witness to the world of the transformative power of your love.

SATURDAY

AM *Psalms: 30, 32*

PM *Psalms: 42, 43*

Ezekiel 39:21–29

John 17:20–26

Philippians 4:10–20

One of my most cherished memories is a conversation I over-heard between my ninety-year-old father and my eighty-seven-year-old mother. We were in a hospital room where Dad was recuperating from a heart procedure. Both of them were frail, and they were obviously deeply concerned about each other. They knew I was there, but in the quiet of the room late at night, I heard them begin to reminisce about their sixty-five years of marriage. I did not engage in the conversation. It was too precious for me to intrude. Their lives had not always been easy. For years health issues had taken a toll on both of them, but I heard not a word of complaint. As I listened there was an intimacy between them I had never had access to before. This was their moment. And, in listening, I discovered things I never dreamed to learn.

The seventeenth chapter of the Gospel of John is central to our Lenten journey. So often we read it as if it were a teaching directed toward the church. In reality, it is an intimate conversation between the Father and his beloved Son. If we listen well, we may discover things we never dreamed to learn.

Jesus is facing the most horrendous experience imaginable. The agony of Gethsemane is before him, where he will pray a different kind of prayer. Ahead will be betrayal, abandonment by his closest friends and followers, arrest, and torture. The bond between the Father and the Son will by ripped at by the intrusion of death. That cry of desperation from the cross, "My God, why have you forsaken me?" takes on massive significance in light of this prayer. Yet, in spite of that specter hovering over the moment, we hear a depth of intimacy expressed in this prayer that we must not overlook.

If we are listening, in our overhearing comes the stunning realization that we are intended to participate in the intimacy Jesus has with the Father. The whole objective toward which Jesus is moving is the restoration of that intimacy between God and us that was formed at creation. And that intimacy with God is the pattern by which we join in relationship with all of those around us.

Lent is intended to lead us into an honest evaluation of our intimacy with the Father. If we will eavesdrop on this conversation, it will confront our independence, our presumption, our arrogant self-absorption. It will drive us to our knees in contrition, in wrenching confession and repentance—all the while holding before us the promise of a depth of intimacy with God and with one another we never dreamed possible.

Be quiet! Just listen.

—JCM

REFLECTION & PRACTICE

01 We are invited into the mutual indwelling of the Father and Son. How might our inclusion in divine intimacy result in witness to the world?

02 Through the indwelling of the triune God in the Christian community, the world comes to see and understand God's deep love.

- Where have you witnessed the fruit of this indwelling in the church?

- Where have you witnessed resistance to the transformative indwelling of God? What was the result of that resistance?

03 Jesus desires for us to experience the love of the Father as he has experienced it.
- How might the experience of being loved deeply by God enable us to engage in Christian community more faithfully?
- What barriers might come down and what brokenness could be restored as we find a home in the love of God?

PRAYER

Lord, thank you for inviting us into the intimacy of the Trinity. We recognize that our inclusion is not only for our sake but also for the sake of the world. Heal our rebellious spirits that strain after independence and self-sufficiency. Forgive our selfish habits that separate us from you and one another. May we humbly allow you to work in us and through us, that the world might know your love.

FIRST SUNDAY IN LENT

AM *Psalms: 63, 98*

PM *Psalm: 103*

Daniel 9:3–10

John 12:44–50

Hebrews 2:10–18

In this Lenten journey you will have opportunity to worship. Hopefully on the day of worship you will gather with a community of faith where you will worship with people who walk with you through this season. During Lent, one of the elements of worship that will benefit us most is the embrace of our own need for grace, mercy, and forgiveness. Corporate confession can be a means of grace.

It is tempting to assume that those who need to repent are "the sinners," people who are "away from God." Or perhaps it is the people in positions of power and authority whose policies we dislike, whose motives we question. Or it is the people whose lifestyles we resent, with whom we hope to have no interaction at all. But in the Daniel text for today, it is righteous Daniel who gives voice to repentance and contrition. He embraces the shame of the status of Israel. They are in exile. The city of Jerusalem has been sacked and burned. It is desolate, and life is bitter for the remnant still eking out a living in the rubble.

Daniel, one of the exiles taken away into captivity, is really in a remarkable situation. He has risen to the status of prime minister and gained much respect and the support of the king. Nevertheless, Daniel identifies himself with the brokenness of Israel. In humility he cries out to the Lord for the restoration of Jerusalem, for God to intervene on behalf of God's people. "We have sinned and done wrong. We have been wicked and have rebelled; we have turned away from your commands and laws" (9:5). "Lord, listen!" he prays. "Lord, forgive! Lord, hear and act!" (v. 19). This is not condemnation of other people. This is not a stance of spiritual superiority. This is a humble embrace of the tragedy of corporate sinfulness that led to the destruction of the temple of God, the city of Jerusalem, and the cohesion of the people of God.

As you prepare for worship, open your heart to our common need for contrition. Read John 12:42, where we are reminded that some of the religious leaders of the day had come to believe that Jesus was worthy of their allegiance but were fearful that their status in the community would be threatened if they dared to identify themselves with him.

Sin's insidious and subtle influence is often hidden beneath the surface of our lives. The power and influence of the people of God for righteousness should have a redemptive impact in every place they are found. But the reality of our nation, our world, and even our religious bodies reveals a destructive silence, a want of transparent and patient holiness that persists even in the face of resistance and scorn.

—JCM

REFLECTION & PRACTICE

01 We often resist confessing our sins to a trusted sister or brother in Christ, assuring ourselves that private confession to God is adequate. But there is no practice that strips away any façade of righteousness faster than confessing sin to a fellow human. Confession initiates a unique spiritual healing in our sin-sick souls (James 5:16) and creates an opportunity for accountability.

- How might you intentionally incorporate the spiritual discipline of confession into your faith practice?
- If you sense a resistance in your spirit to this challenge, pause and explore that response, asking the Holy Spirit for clarity and guidance.

02 Daniel's corporate confession unsettles us. Daniel was not likely committing heinous acts of idolatry himself. Yet he recognized and acknowledged his part in a system characterized by evil, a system that worked against the purposes of God and against God's intent for human flourishing. We too participate in systems that perpetuate inequality, racism, misogyny, xenophobia, and cyclical poverty.

- What might it look like in your life to join Daniel in corporate confession and humbly acknowledge your place in the brokenness all around us?
- With careful intent, listen to the stories of those who are different from you without taking a posture of defensiveness. Take seriously stories of hurt, exclusion, and hopelessness.
- Ask the Spirit to open your eyes to injustice around you and how you might embody the kingdom of God in that situation.

PRAYER

Lord, we acknowledge that, in service to our pride and ego, we often avoid the discipline of confession. We guard our public perception, thereby strengthening the chains of habitual sin by keeping them hidden from our sisters and brothers. Give us courage to confess, both with careful discernment and vulnerable boldness. Forgive us also for our fixation on our individual spiritual status that often blinds us to our participation in broken, evil systems that stand as an affront to you and your desire for human flourishing. Give us eyes to see, ears to listen, and hearts ready and willing to obey whatever you might ask of us. Make us agents of reconciliation and transformation.

MONDAY

AM *Psalms: 41, 52*

PM *Psalm: 44*

Genesis 37:1–11

Mark 1:1–13

1 Corinthians 1:1–19

In the Genesis account of creation, God spoke into the chaos of formlessness and darkness, with the strong wind of God blowing across the waters. At God's word, light broke into the darkness. God's good creation burst into being. It was good. It was very good. But in the beauty of creation lurked a potential for chaos that soon raised its ugly head. With the willful and high-handed disobedience of Adam and Eve came an angry chaos that distorted everything God had made. But God was not done with creation. The loving, determined persistence of God addressed the chaos, creating an avenue through which, in time, the chaos would be reversed.

In the Gospel of Mark, God begins again. But the story of God's new beginning immediately encounters chaos. Sin, repentance, confession. People are baptized, washed in water. It is dramatic and chaotic. Even Jesus, the Son of God, is baptized. And, reminiscent of the account of creation, the Spirit descends over the waters! But immediately afterward, the Spirit drives Jesus into the wilderness where, for forty days, he is confronted by Satan, tempted, tortured, and surrounded by danger and wild animals. At end of the forty days, according to the Gospel of Luke, Satan left him "until an opportune time" (Luke 4:13).

Chaos had not ended. Jesus dealt with it throughout his ministry—facing it, confronting it, condemning it. But the nearer Jesus drew to Jerusalem on that final journey, the more chaos revealed its fury. It culminated in that final cry from the lips of Jesus on the cross: "It is finished" (John 19:30).

In the prayer of Jesus recorded in John 17, Jesus prayed for his disciples with these words: "My prayer is not that you take them out of the world but that you protect them from the evil one" (v. 15). In that prayer Jesus acknowledged two realities. The first was that chaos was doomed! With that final cry from the cross, all the powers of sin, death, and hell were ultimately defeated. The other thing Jesus acknowledged was that, in the interim between the death and resurrection of Jesus and the return of Jesus to restore all of creation to the beauty and perfection originally intended, chaos would seek to reassert its dominion over creation and humanity. The resurrection of Jesus made it clear that the power of chaos is broken. It may still rear its ugly head at times, but it is broken, defeated, overcome. It will eventually be eliminated.

In the meantime, as our Lenten journey reminds us, we have to deal with chaos. It is real. It is painful. It is disruptive. And it is at times agonizing. But it is not final. When chaos rears its ugly head, lean into Jesus!

—JCM

REFLECTION & PRACTICE

01 In various eras throughout recorded history, humankind has become so impressed with our own accomplishments that we have bought into the lie that chaos can be eliminated through human diligence and perseverance. Disease can be eradicated, wars rendered obsolete, poverty eliminated.

- Where do you see this idolatrous narrative at work?
- In what ways is this confidence in humanity an affront to the gospel?
- What are the resulting behaviors of this view?

02 In contrast to the idolatrous optimism of progressive humanism, those who have experienced the persistence of poverty, the evil of violence, and the greed and abuse of the powerful have a different perspective. There is no hope. Humankind is trapped by the chaos all around. The best one can hope for is a decent life with minimal pain and an easy death.

- Where do you see this despair and hopelessness at work around you?
- How is this perspective equally opposed to the gospel?
- What are the resulting behaviors of this view?

03 There is a more faithful way that rejects both idolatrous optimism and despair. It is the way of the in-breaking kingdom of God. We acknowledge the reality of chaos and our inability to quell the forces of evil by sheer force and ingenuity, but we also acknowledge that sin and death have been cut off at the root as the kingdom of God has broken into creation. Death shall die, and we shall live with Christ.

- What might it look like to live faithfully in this tension?
- How do we avoid the extremes of passivity and self-righteous activism?
- How can we resist both despair and idolatrous self-sufficiency and instead embrace an intimate partnership with God?

PRAYER

Lord, we cannot deny the chaos around us. Creation itself groans with longing for redemption. Because of what you have done in Christ, we reject despair and resignation. We also repent of our idolatrous attempts to untangle the chaos through our own strength. We humbly acknowledge you as the source of redemption and reconciliation, and we accept your call to join you in that restorative work as we await the moment when your kingdom will come in its fullness. Empower us to live as faithful, obedient citizens of your in-breaking kingdom now.

TUESDAY

AM *Psalm: 45*

PM *Psalms: 47, 48*

Genesis 37:12–24

Mark 1:14–28

1 Corinthians 1:20–31

Had I been choosing the disciples of Jesus I might have chosen a more impressive group than fishermen, tax collectors, and zealots. What kind of religious movement could you possibly build on the shoulders of people like that? The same thought seems to have crossed the mind of the apostle Paul. To use a more contemporary term, the people who made up the church in Corinth seemed like a "basket of deplorables." Not wise by human standards, not influential, not of noble birth.

Our devaluation of other humans can be brutal. Our assessments of their capacity are sometimes a subtle distaste at having been overlooked or not selected ourselves. As my friend Dr. Chuck Crow once said to me after my election to a position of responsibility, "Have you ever noticed that when your friend is elected to high office, you don't think more of your friend? You think less of the office."

Both Jesus and Paul challenge our assumptions and evaluations. Our measurements often see only the surface and draw conclusions that are both unwarranted and potentially destructive. Jesus saw in Simon a potential rock on which the church could be founded. Paul observed that God chose the weak things, the despised things, to shame the world. The jealous brothers of Joseph had blinded themselves to what God was attempting to accomplish through their own family on behalf of God's people, Israel. And the synagogue in Capernaum was likely filled with people who were disgusted that Jesus would spend time dealing with a person who could well have been a perpetual source of embarrassment for them all.

On a recent Sunday morning the women's choir from the Kansas City Rescue Mission sang as part of our worship experience. Coming from many manifestations of utter brokenness, they held up cardboard signs with one-word summaries of their various backgrounds. Words like: Addiction. Slavery. Alcoholism. Homelessness. As they sang their original song, composed with the help of a member of the staff at the Mission, their signs were turned over: Deliverance. Freedom. Sobriety. Home! No longer defined by their brokenness, now they sang a song of deliverance and freedom, transformed by Christ's profound love and mercy. How Jesus saw them transformed them.

What might happen if we saw people with the eyes of Jesus? How might our journey through Lent tamp down our temptation toward disdain of others? As Jesus approached Jerusalem there was an obvious narrowing of the agenda. Those last hours were spent with the disciples, pouring himself into them, shaping their understanding of what was to come. Knowing the likelihood that they were all going to desert him, he still poured himself into them, knowing what could be. Maybe the point of Lent is leaning enough into Jesus that we see people not as they are but as they could be! Lean in. Pour out.

—JCM

REFLECTION & PRACTICE

01 We eagerly welcome God's merciful inclusion of us yet often struggle to imagine the same welcome extended to others we deem inferior to or in "worse shape" than ourselves. Relational distance from such as these makes such judgments even more pronounced.

- Which individuals or groups of people in your life tend to elicit negative, judgment-laden assessments?
- What might happen if you sought out connection and practiced empathy instead of passing judgment or keeping yourself apart?

02 The hope of holiness is the promise that, through the work of the Spirit and our responsive obedience, we need not—*cannot*—stay as we are. We are invited into an increasingly spacious place of freedom in which we are free both from the need to defend ourselves and the need to measure ourselves against others.

- In what areas of your life do you find yourself defensive or protective? Consider inviting someone you trust to help you see yourself clearly.
- What would it look like to continually rest in your beloved-ness?
- How might this attitude transform your relationships?

PRAYER

Lord, thank you that you have chosen the weak things of this world to shame the strong. Our gratitude to you for inviting us into your family overflows. However, we acknowledge that—out of fear, self-protection, and judgment—we often fail to extend that same hospitality to others. We confess our eagerness to be included while actively excluding others through our judgments and lack of empathy. Cleanse us from these unholy attitudes and patterns. Thank you that you do not leave us as we are but call us forward into true and holy life, empowered by the Spirit.

WEDNESDAY

AM *Psalm: 119:49–72*

PM *Psalms: 49, 53*

Genesis 37:25–36

Mark 1:29–45

1 Corinthians 2:1–13

The Lenten journey occurs during a season that is characterized by busyness. In the U.S. and Canada, spring is beginning, schools are looking toward the end of the school year, and preparations for Easter crowd the schedule for pastors and church leaders. That schedule does not lend itself to reflection, prayer, service to others, or self-denial. Who or what is setting your Lenten agenda?

Today's Gospel passage describes a packed schedule for Jesus. Leaving the synagogue where so much has just happened, Jesus is confronted by the illness of Simon's mother-in-law. With gentle compassion he heals her, and she begins to serve them all. By the end of the day the whole town is gathered at the door of the home. There are sick people and those who are demon-possessed. The pressure must be intense. It is little wonder that Jesus makes his way, early in the morning, to a solitary place. He needs some space. He needs time to pray. He needs to draw from his Father the resources for the increasing demands on his time and energy. The disciples begin to search desperately for him. They presume to know the agenda he should follow. "Everyone is looking for you!" they tell him (Mark 1:37).

He says, "Let's go somewhere else. There are other villages where I need to preach."

He went throughout Galilee, preaching in their synagogues, driving out demons, healing diseases. He encountered a man who had leprosy, had mercy on him, and healed him. Jesus expressly told him: "Don't tell this to anyone." He instructed him instead to go to the priest and offer the sacrifices Moses commanded. This was to be a testimony that the God of Moses was still at work. But the man, again presuming to know the agenda Jesus should follow, told everyone that Jesus had healed him. As a result, Jesus could no longer go into the villages and teach in the synagogues. He had to stay in the lonely places.

When we become amateur providences—when we presume to know how God should fulfill the agenda we have for God—we so often hinder the objective toward which God is moving. Jesus could no longer do what he expressly desired to do because the man who had been healed chose to believe he knew better.

One of the objectives of Lent is to set us free from our dependence on frenetic busyness. One of our greatest goals should be that, during a season when the pressure to *do* increases with every passing day, we intentionally set aside time for solitude, prayer and fasting, and spiritual renewal.

—JCM

REFLECTION & PRACTICE

01 In our culture, busyness is often treated as a badge of honor indicating a person's importance. With the additional pressure to pursue success and the accompanying external indicators, we find ourselves bogged down with cluttered hearts, minds, and homes.

  - Where do you see the lie of busyness as importance at work in your life?
  - What underlying fears or expectations might be fueling that lie?

02 Lent is a season of intentional paring down, releasing what might be *good* in order to make room for what is *best*.

- In conversation with your loved ones, take an honest look at the clutter in your lives. What eats up your time? Are possessions consuming your energy? What activities or commitments prevent you from being present with those you love and with God? Are any financial obligations paralyzing you?
- Challenge yourself and your family to experiment.
    i. What habits or commitments can be eliminated or limited? Take a social media or TV hiatus. Invite your children to choose only one or two extracurricular activities.
    ii. Have a purge party and see who can come up with the most excess to give away.
    iii. Take a hard look at your financial commitments. Wrestle honestly with what you need as opposed to what you want or what provides social status.
- Practice the discipline of holy imagination. With this new margin in your life, what might be possible?

PRAYER

Lord, we confess our idolatry of busyness. We often participate in the lie that our busyness indicates our importance or value. Forgive us for the ways in which we have filled our lives with good things at the expense of the best things. We long for liberation from the excess. Give us the courage to be honest with ourselves as we seek to align our lives with the way of your kingdom, that we might experience the freedom only you can give.

THURSDAY

AM *Psalms: 50, 59, 60*

PM *Psalms: 19, 46*

Genesis 39:1–23

Mark 2:1–12

1 Corinthians 2:14–3:15

In our Gospel passage, it is the early days of Jesus's ministry, but he has already sent waves rippling through Galilee. Unclean spirits have been banished, the sick have been healed, and even a leper has been cleansed. When Jesus returns to Capernaum, it is no wonder people swarm to him. Who is this man who speaks and acts with an authority unlike anything they have ever witnessed?

Enter a group of devoted and determined friends, along with their paralyzed companion. Not to be deterred by a house packed to bursting, four friends somehow ascend the roof and get to work making an alternative entrance by *removing* the roof. This is not a polite, unobtrusive gesture, but neither physical nor social barriers will deter them from their mission of attaining wholeness for their friend. The shock at seeing a man lowered through a roof is great but pales in comparison to the shock to come.

Jesus sees the faith of the friends, looks at the paralyzed man, and declares, "Son, your sins are forgiven" (Mark 2:5). Who is more shocked now—the scribes who know that "God alone" can forgive sins (v. 7) or the man on the mat, anticipating physical healing but receiving instead the restoration of his soul? As they sit in stunned silence, mouths agape, Jesus acts yet again. To demonstrate his authority to forgive sins, Jesus calls out to the man on the mat, "Get up, take your mat and go home" (v. 11). The man rises, healed and whole inside and out.

To those who have heard the story before, and the numerous other stories of Jesus's healings, the conclusion is not surprising. But this particular healing stands apart. In no other story do we witness the faith of a group of friends as displayed in this story. The dramatic roof removal is remarkable and even endearing, but it demonstrates more than persistence and ingenuity. When Jesus looks at the friends, the text says he sees their faith—not the faith of the man on the mat but the faith of his companions. Their faith on behalf of their friend prompts Jesus to act, declaring the young man's sins to be forgiven.

In cultures where we are so fixated on independence and autonomy, the idea that our faith is intimately interwoven with the faith of the Christian community is uncomfortable. We fancy ourselves self-sufficient and self-reliant. *Jesus and me is all I need.* But the man on the mat knows differently. Not only can he not physically bring himself to Jesus, but the text also stirs our imagination to wonder if perhaps his faith cannot spiritually bring him to Jesus either. Perhaps he is plagued by despair or heavily burdened by the weight of his sin. Perhaps he is consumed by doubt, feeling unloved and forgotten by God. We cannot know, but we do know that in some mysterious and holy way, the faith of his friends results in the young man's encounter with salvation in the flesh, resulting in freedom from sin and death as well as freedom from his ailment.

As we journey toward the cross this Lenten season, may we surrender the idolatrous narrative of self-sufficiency and autonomy. May we trust and believe on behalf of our sisters and brothers who are struggling under the weight of sin, doubt, and fear. But may we also abandon our pride and allow our Christian community to trust and believe on our behalf when we are weary and cannot see the path before us. Together, may we bring one another to Jesus.

—SDL

REFLECTION & PRACTICE

01 This is one of the most widely recognized stories of healing in the Gospels. It is a remarkable story, filled with nuances and unexpected turns. It can be so familiar, however, that we can miss its power.

- What in this story catches your attention first? Where does it differ from other healing stories?
- What do you imagine was the initial response of the people crowded around Jesus?

02 The man on the mat was incapable of making his way to Jesus. The tenacious effort of friends was his only hope.

- What possibly motivated the friends to take such dramatic steps to get their friend before Jesus? Where do you picture yourself in the event? In the crowd? On the mat? Digging through the roof? Why?
- In what way might you be in a position similar to that of the friends of the man on the mat? What would you do?

03 Jesus obviously sees the condition of the man being lowered in front of him. He also immediately recognizes the faith of the friends.

- Why do you think Jesus begins his response to their efforts by declaring the man forgiven? Where does Jesus place the greatest emphasis in this event? What does that say to our efforts at helping people?
- How does this event inform our need for one another?

PRAYER

Lord, our self-sufficiency often hinders our ability to depend on those around us when our own resources of faith, hope, and security are at greatest risk. Thank you for the promise that we who follow you are not left to our own resources. We have you, and for that we are grateful. But help us realize the resource we also have in one another. Help us realize the resource we can be to one another. May we be avenues of grace for those around us who most need your help.

FRIDAY

AM *Psalms: 40, 54*

PM *Psalm: 51*

Genesis 40:1–23

Mark 2:13–22

1 Corinthians 3:16–23

Ambivalence and ambiguity often seem to characterize the lives of Christians in our culture. Uncertainty over what is essential, tension over how Christians define holiness, and confusion over how believers are to relate to the brokenness around us all raise many questions.

Mark tells us that Jesus eating at the home of Levi the tax collector brings strong criticism from the teachers of the law who are Pharisees. The ease with which many Christians identify the Pharisees as narrow and legalistic misses a very important part of the ambiguity of this passage. The Pharisees are not priests or temple servants. They are laypeople—deeply committed folk who take the law of God seriously and who believe deeply that holiness should mean something to a true Israelite. The Pharisees love the law. They do not see it as an imposition or as mere legalistic observance. They think that if God is holy, God's people should be holy.

For Jesus, the issue is not that the Pharisees are wrong. The issue is that the law was intended to form a life characterized by love of neighbor, which meant that holiness was not intended to draw lines of demarcation between holy people and sinners. Jesus is the representation of the Father and the fulfillment of the law. The way of Jesus—reaching out to the sick and communing with and calling the sinners—is the way of God, the way of the law. For Jesus, the tragedy of the Pharisees is their blindness to their own need for grace and mercy. Jesus gathering with sinners and tax collectors is not seen by the Pharisees as a sign of the in-breaking kingdom. Their growing antagonism toward Jesus demonstrates a callous disregard for the scandalous love of God for the outcasts.

The Lenten journey is for believers. It is a season when our own hearts and minds should be under the microscope. It is a season when our spirit should be under examination by the Spirit of God and the Word for any arrogance and self-righteousness. In fasting and self-denial, we seek to examine our motives to discern whether we have assumed a judgmental or harshly critical position toward the weaknesses, sins, or foibles of another. What we discover should be faced with the humility and contrition found in Psalm 51.

Does holiness matter? Yes! Certainly! But holiness is not best measured by a set of practices by which we curry God's favor or impress those who observe us. Holiness is cultivated in humility. Holiness is participation in the very life of Christ by the Spirit. Holiness is the love of God flowing into and through us toward the broken, the struggling, the addicted, and the hungry. Those despised tax collectors and sinners are drawn to the transparent love and holiness of Jesus. Their sin does not contaminate his holiness. Their brokenness does not diminish his love. That reality was and still is scandalous!

—JCM

REFLECTION & PRACTICE

01 When you read the Mark text, with which group in the story do you initially identify? Levi and the other sinners? Or the Pharisees? Explore empathy for both groups.

- As a tax collector, how might it feel to be included by Jesus after being excluded by your own people?

- As a Pharisee, how might it feel to see rebellious, disobedient fellow Jews receiving what appears to be special favor from this unique teacher? What reaction might this seemingly unjust behavior on the part of Jesus incite in you?

02 The problem with the Pharisees is not their diagnosis of the sin-sickness in others; it is their blindness to their own need of a doctor. When Jesus announces that he has come not for the righteous but for sinners, he is not excluding the Pharisees; he is calling out their self-righteousness as false and empty.

- How does our fixation with the sins of others blind us to the sin at work in our own hearts?
- Why does Jesus's radical inclusion of outsiders often elicit defensiveness in us, the insiders?

03 "Holiness is the love of God flowing into and through us." Love is often interpreted as a soft, agreeable posture in which we passively extend warm feelings and refrain from judgment. But love demands action. Love that does not result in a heart moved to compassion and hands moved to work for the healing and transformation of others is not love.

- In what areas of your life might God be inviting you to actively love the broken, despised, and rejected?
- What challenges would you face in practicing that active love? Misunderstanding from others? The need to let go of other activities to make space and time?

PRAYER

Lord, we confess our preoccupation with the external indicators of holiness at the expense of practicing holy love. We are often so consumed by determining who is in and who is out that we fail to see our own hearts drifting from you. We acknowledge once again that our righteousness is but filthy rags. Only by you and through you do we come to God. In humility, we admit our desperate need of a doctor for our sin-sick souls. In your great love for us, set us free from the chains of legalism and boundary-enforcing in order that we might love the hurting, the poor, the broken, and the afraid with the love with which you have loved us. May our lives bear witness to your holy, transformative love.

SATURDAY

AM *Psalm: 55*

PM *Psalms: 138, 139*

Genesis 41:1–13

Mark 2:23–3:6

1 Corinthians 4:1–7

Sacred time and sacred space can sometimes be confusing practices to navigate. Sabbath observance was obviously important to the ancient people of God. Strict guidelines were given for what could be done on the seventh day of the week that would be in keeping with the rest God experienced after the work of creation. God instructed us to "keep the Sabbath." Over time, rabbis added rules and regulations that governed nearly every movement or activity in response to questions about how one was to practice Sabbath while living in the real world. One of the most difficult aspects of keeping the Sabbath became knowing what all the rules were.

The sacred precincts of the temple gave the appropriate people access to various courtyards within the temple grounds. There was the temple courtyard for the men and another beyond it for the women. Gentiles were hindered from ever approaching the sacred inner sanctum.

They were restricted to the outer courtyard of the gentiles. The Holy of Holies—that most sacred space at the very center of the temple—was accessible only once a year to the high priest.

In our own era, especially in the Holiness tradition, there were sincere attempts to define Sabbath-keeping so the day would be protected for worship and rest. In our sanctuaries, humble as they often were, children were told not to run or shout or play on the altar.

In Mark's account in today's reading, two events occur where Jesus is confronted for his apparent disregard for the tradition of Sabbath keeping. His disciples, walking through grain fields (perhaps even walking a greater distance than the rules allow) are seen plucking heads of grain, probably rubbing the grain between their hands to remove the chaff, and tossing the grain into their mouths.

"They are doing what is unlawful on the Sabbath," cry the Pharisees! In a brief word, reiterated in the later event where Jesus heals a man with a withered hand, he makes it clear that humanity was not made to keep the Sabbath but that the Sabbath was made to keep—to protect, refresh, sustain—humankind. The Sabbath is a good time. It is not a time for demand and restriction but a time for life, healing, confession, grace, embrace, joy, laughter.

By this time, our observance of the Lenten journey could have become a task. Continuing to keep Lent could become a burden if we are not careful. But keep this before you: you are not called to keep Lent. Lent is designed to keep you! This is for your sake. The Lenten season is a time to draw near to a God who passionately loves you, has provided abundantly more grace than you can imagine, and who seeks to draw near to you. Let Lent keep you!

—JCM

REFLECTION & PRACTICE

01 Our perception of the Sabbath is heavily shaped by our first experience with it. The attitudes and behaviors of those around us influence how we understand this command of God. In our attempts to bring the command to life, we have often reduced the gift to specific do's and don'ts.

- How did you first experience Sabbath? Did you experience it as a gift or as a burden?

- How do you currently obey the command to practice Sabbath? Are there Jesus followers in your life whom you respect and trust who might offer practical suggestions?

02 When the religious leaders refuse to respond to Jesus's inquiry about whether doing good or healing actually breaks the Sabbath, Jesus is angry but also deeply grieved. How tragic that God's command, given to protect and serve God's people, is turned into a weapon of judgment and control.
- What good gifts of God do we misuse for our own purposes?
- How might we, like the well-intentioned religious leaders, grieve God when we harden our hearts against the good intentions undergirding God's commands?
- The religious leaders' harsh interpretation of God's command was most harmful to the vulnerable. How might our self-centered religious convictions do damage to the vulnerable instead of give life?

03 Humankind was not made to keep the Sabbath; the Sabbath was made to keep humankind. God, in God's wisdom and foresight, knew we needed protection from ourselves and from the idolatrous lie that we are the source of life.
- How might the Sabbath keep you? What freedom, rest, and joy might you experience if you allowed the Sabbath to care for you instead of seeking to serve it?

PRAYER

Lord, thank you for the gift of the Sabbath. We confess that often we have not received it as a gift. We have treated your provision as a burden and even as a weapon to control and manipulate others. Forgive us for not trusting your heart. May we learn to trust you more deeply and allow your gift of the Sabbath to keep us.

SECOND SUNDAY IN LENT

AM *Psalms: 24, 29*

PM *Psalms: 8, 84*

Genesis 41:14–45

John 5:19–24

Romans 6:3–14

Everyone loves a good reconciliation story: a relationship that was shattered is restored through repentance and forgiveness. It's no wonder that the parable of the prodigal son is so well known even beyond the community of faith. We rejoice when the son comes to his senses, and we rejoice all the more when the father extends radical mercy, welcoming the son back home. What if, after settling back into his old room and getting some meat back on his wasted frame, the son decides, "Well, I'm feeling better. But I'm missing some of my party buddies. I think I'll go back and give the party life another go." Without a second thought, the son rifles through his mom's purse for cash and heads back out on the road. We are horrified by the suggestion. How dare he—after all he's been given! How dare he treat the mercy and grace of his father with such disdain!

In the epistle passage today, Paul addresses this pattern he sees among the followers of Jesus—this idea that, since we can count on the grace of Jesus Christ, maybe it's okay to keep living selfishly and sinfully because the grace of Jesus will cover us! Paul makes it clear that such thinking is a perversion of God's grace. In *The Cost of Discipleship,* twentieth-century theologian and martyr Dietrich Bonhoeffer describes this kind of thinking as cheap grace. He talks about how cheap grace doesn't change our lives. "Everything can remain as it was before" because, Bonhoeffer says, the account was "paid in advance." Our card has been punched for that reward in the sky, so let's live as we please until then!

Not so, say both Paul and Bonhoeffer. Everything has changed. Nothing can be as it was before. When we were plunged into the waters of baptism, we died to our old lives. We surrendered our citizenship to the land of death and abandoned our lives there. When we were raised up out of the water, we entered a new land where Christ reigns supreme. We are one with Christ in death and life, and we are invited into a new way of being that points to the coming kingdom of God. For this reason, we reject the siren call of sin, always trying to lure us back to that old land, that old way of being. But we don't live there any more. Now we give ourselves fully to this kingdom way of being. Every part of our lives is dedicated to God's service because God is the one who has brought us from death to life.

This Lenten season, we reject cheap grace and its hollow promises and, instead, give ourselves fully to the transformative grace of God, wrought by the waters of baptism. At times, the enemy will whisper lies trying to convince us that we are still slaves, still beholden to that old way of being. But we are not in Adam; we are in Christ and thus a new creation, raised up with Christ to walk in the newness of life.

—SDL

REFLECTION & PRACTICE

01 As believers, we have been reconciled to God. There is no better description of our new relationships with God and with others. God's abundant provision of grace has altered everything.

- How has your relationship with God changed? In what ways are you now living a new life?
- What has God's gift of righteousness meant to you in your journey with Christ and with others?

02 "Everything has changed. Nothing can be as it was before." Those words challenge the assumption that we are free to live as we please now that we are forgiven. Paul makes a clear and unequivocal statement: "We are those who have died to sin" (Romans 6:2).

- What does it mean to say that we have died to sin? What has Christ accomplished for and in us that gives meaning to that statement?
- Free grace is offered to us. What bearing might that gift have on our conduct or choices?

03 If you have been baptized, Paul says you were baptized into Christ's death, in order that you may live a new life. The power of sin to enslave us has been broken. We have "been set free from sin" (Romans 6:7).

- What does this suggest about what God has done for us?
- Does this mean we will no longer face temptation or failure?
- When the enemy of our souls challenges us, confuses us, or tempts us to despair, what practices might help us remain rooted in the confidence of our salvation?

PRAYER

Father, as we continue this Lenten journey, we are grateful for the reminder that we have been reconciled to God through the death of your son. But we are also reminded, sometimes graphically, that to have been reconciled does not mean the end of our liability to temptation and failure. Thank you for the reminder today that we who have been baptized into Christ's death are raised to new life. Teach us to rely on your grace, in the power of your Spirit, and to live responsibly as we seek to reflect your goodness and love to those around us.

MONDAY

AM *Psalms: 56, 57, 58*

PM *Psalms: 64, 65*

Genesis 41:46–57

Mark 3:7–19a

1 Corinthians 4:8–21

God is always at work. There is not a time or a place where God is not at work. All the time. Everywhere. With everyone. Just yesterday, on the first day of the week—the traditional day of worship for most—Christian believers across the globe gathered to worship. But God's work was not limited to those gatherings. God was at work everywhere, with everyone. Even among those who did not know or acknowledge God, God was at work—wooing, calling, confronting, seeking to draw others to himself.

In Mark's Gospel, the people who were crowding in around Jesus came from far and near, some traveling a hundred miles or more. Some were from the Jewish heartland. Others were from predominantly gentile areas. It is altogether possible that some of those who were pressing in on him were "outsiders," those who were likely looked down upon by the Pharisees as unworthy to be seen or touched by Jesus.

The psalmist sings the expanse of the love and passion of God: "I will praise you, Lord, among the nations; I will sing of you among the peoples. For great is your love, reaching to the heavens; your faithfulness reaches to the skies" (57:9–10). To see an astonishing demonstration of the faithfulness and love of God for all people, look again at Genesis 41:57: "And all the world came to Egypt to buy grain from Joseph, because the famine was severe everywhere."

One of the great dangers of our Christian journey is the tendency to become so focused on our own spiritual health and so preoccupied with who is in and who is out that we fail to recognize the passionate love of God for everyone. The scandal of Jesus's message is his insistence that he came not just for the Jews but also for the whole world (John 3:16). The disciples were shocked to see Jesus conversing with a Samaritan woman. They were stunned to hear that there were "other sheep," folk not of their (Jewish) flock (John 10:16).

In preparation for the proper celebration of an Easter morning, we must become overwhelmed with the expanse of the love and passion of God for everyone, everywhere, all the time. The disciples and the followers of Jesus were so fixated on their expectation that the Messiah's purpose was to redeem Israel that they entirely missed the intent that this Jewish Messiah was to be the world's Redeemer! Dig deeper. Don't miss the point: Everyone. Everywhere. Always.

—JCM

REFLECTION & PRACTICE

01 God is at work at all times, in all people, everywhere. The Spirit of God continually pursues us in love for our good.

- Where have you seen God moving in expected and unexpected places?
- How is the realization of God's persistent pursuit of us both a word of grace, hope, and relief *and* at the same time a call to action?

02 Consider the first time you became aware of God's great love for you.

- Who embodied the love of God to you in a way that you understood?

- How has the realization of God's love for and pursuit of you changed how you see yourself and the world?

03 The church is God's chosen method of working in the world. Through the infilling of the Holy Spirit, we are called and empowered to embody God's radical, transformative love that chases after even the most wayward sheep.
- Who are the excluded, lost, and wounded sheep in your sphere of influence?
- How might you embody the persistent, passionate love of God to the unlovable and excluded in your world?

04 Many of Jesus's followers failed to recognize God's intent to save all of creation, so focused were they on what they desired for themselves.
- In what ways do we become so focused on the individual benefits of salvation that we fail to see the larger redemptive work God is doing around us?
- How might we posture ourselves in such a way as to be more attentive to how God is working to redeem all people in all places, and even creation itself?

PRAYER

Lord, we give you praise and thanks for your tenacious love, your dogged pursuit of us, and your unflagging faithfulness even in the face of our faithlessness. We confess that, in our delight at experiencing your love and inclusion, we often lose sight of those still in need of your transformative love. You have blessed us to be a blessing. Forgive us when we neglect that call. As Jesus healed so many sightless ones, heal us of our spiritual blindness, that we might see clearly those around us and their need. May we love as we have been loved: without measure.

TUESDAY

AM *Psalms: 61, 62*

PM *Psalm: 68*

Genesis 42:1–17

Mark 3:20–35

1 Corinthians 5:1–8

The risk of following Jesus is that it may rearrange reality for you, which is neither easy nor comfortable, but it has been the experience of those who follow Jesus passionately since the very beginning. Modern culture defines reality in terms of power, position, or possessions. Those matters become the focus of life, the measure of success, and the source of our security. It should not surprise us that when we begin to passionately follow Jesus, there are many, including family and friends, who will question our wisdom and challenge our priorities. Even the family of Jesus was concerned that he was "out of his mind" (Mark 3:21). When the circumstances of life create anguish, pain, or uncertainty, the pragmatism of many Christians relies more on what is perceived as reality in the culture than on what it means to have an intimate relationship with Jesus.

A young man attended a district youth camp and came into a transforming relationship with Jesus Christ. On his return home his family, deeply involved in their local church, were thrilled. Over the next two years, as he neared graduation from high school, he began to testify to a call from God to go into Christian ministry. When he became seriously invested in attending a Christian university in order to prepare for ministry, his father and mother became agitated and critical. They made an appointment with their pastor, expressing their anger that the plans they had for their son were being undermined by his "pipe dream."

"What possible future could he have as a pastor?" his father asked. "This is just a crazy idea."

It took a while, but the young man, who remained deeply respectful of his parents, saw them come to a place of surrender to a better vision of reality than they had been willing to consider. Today that young man is a fruitful and faithful pastor, leading a congregation serving the lost and broken people in an urban center. His parents are among the most faithful prayer warriors for his ministry.

In Psalms 61 and 62, David—surrounded by threat and pressure— has found reality. "You have given me the heritage of those who fear your name," he cries (61:5). "My salvation and my honor depend on God" (62:7).

Perhaps your Lenten journey will enable you to get a new grasp on reality. Perhaps it is an opportunity for you to *really* follow Jesus.

—JCM

REFLECTION & PRACTICE

01 We often look on fanatics with disdain, and often for valid reasons. Fanaticism frequently results in violence—both physical and spiritual—as well as blindness to any perspective differing from one's own. The focus becomes the devotion of the fanatic over and above the object of devotion.

- What is the difference between fanaticism and radical obedience?
- Philosopher George Santayana defined fanaticism as "redoubling your effort when you have forgotten your aim." In our commitment to practice unwavering faithfulness in the midst of a faithless world, how do we ensure we do not forget our aim?

02 The young man in today's devotional was faithful to a call, even before his family could understand God's call on his life. As we seek to listen and obey the call of the Lord, even those who love us most might not stand in agreement with us.

- How might we navigate the tension that often exists between the opinions of others and the call of the Lord?
- What are some safeguards we can put into place that will protect us from pride and ego, while still giving us space to explore the unexpected call of God?
- Consider finding a spiritual director—someone who is not personally invested in your life like a parent but is trained to assist individuals in discerning the voice of the Spirit from the voice of others and the voice of the ego.

PRAYER

Lord, our deepest desire is to follow you faithfully. We confess we are easily distracted by the competing voices around us, all claiming to know what is best for us. Grant us the discernment to hear your voice and, with humility, receive the counsel of those we trust. Ultimately, give us the courage to obey regardless of the cost. You are worthy of our trust. Our future is never more secure than when placed in your hands.

WEDNESDAY

AM *Psalm: 72*

PM *Psalm: 119:73–96*

Genesis 42:18–28

Mark 4:1–20

1 Corinthians 5:6–6:8

Lent is not intended for casual engagement with God. It is a summons to discipleship at a deep and transformative level. It could well be uncomfortable for many of us. Perhaps it should be for many more of us. That is the lesson of Mark 4:1–20. This is a difficult parable to interpret. Is this parable about the sower, who went out to sow, throwing seed widely, generously, indiscriminately, not heeding the readiness or preparation of the soil? That could sound like good news. That looks a lot like grace! Or is this parable about the soil and the variety of responses to the message of Jesus?

He is speaking to a crowd that has gathered from all over the region. How could they be described? Desperate for a fix, for a miraculous intervention, for healing for themselves or a family member or friend? Maybe some are just curious. "Who is this miracle worker? Let's go see what will happen today." Are some of them gripped by the realization that this man Jesus just might be the long-awaited Messiah of Israel?

Without explanation, Jesus simply tells the story and then concludes by saying, "Listen carefully."

The Twelve and others around him who seem interested in what he has to say are confused. What does he mean with this parable? Whom is he referring to? What does this story mean for them?

"Help us," they say. "What were you talking about?"

Parables are not intended to be heard intellectually. They are intended to speak viscerally. The meaning does not easily unfold. You must listen deeply. Even then, it is not easy to know. Unless you are willing to be shaped by the story you are hearing, you can miss it. How you listen matters. In his explanation, Jesus returns to the theme with which, according to the Gospel of Mark, he began his preaching ministry: "'The time has come,' he said. 'The kingdom of God has come near. Repent and believe the good news!'" (Mark 1:15). Now, in his explanation of the parable of the sower, he begins by saying to them, "The secret of the kingdom of God has been given to you" (Mark 4:11).

Repent. Turn around. Reorient your life. Go in a different direction. Get serious about where you are headed and how you got where you are. "Listen carefully," says Jesus. "Get this right."

—JCM

REFLECTION & PRACTICE

01 Parables cannot be decoded; their meaning must be revealed. Logic cannot save us, nor right thinking deliver us. In Psalm 119:73, the psalmist says, "Give me understanding to learn your commands."

- How does this instruction offer a corrective to the common assumption that we can deduce the mind of the Lord?
- In humility, Jesus's followers asked for understanding. Is there a need for renewed humility in your heart, a reorientation to the role of learner?

02 "How you listen matters." Our posture toward the Word and the illuminating Spirit of God often parallels the soils in this familiar parable.

- Is it possible to embody each of these soils at different times in our lives? Reflect on the soil seasons throughout your faith journey.
- How would you describe your current posture toward the Lord? Sensitive and eager to listen and obey? Distracted and apathetic? Quick to say yes but easily discouraged when hardship arises?
- Is there a need for repentance in your life? Where might God be inviting you to go a new way?

03 When read as the parable of the Sower, what does this story reveal about the character of God? In what ways does this revelation of God differ from how we often understand God's way in the world?

04 As co-laborers in the work of redemption, what might it look like to practice the extravagant generosity of the sower? What needs to change in our approach toward others who are in need of the transforming grace of God?

PRAYER

Lord, in humility we acknowledge that we often look but do not perceive; we listen but do not understand. In our arrogance and familiarity, we presume to know your heart and mind. We repent and return to you, asking that you unveil our eyes and hearts that we might understand and obey. Thank you for the gift of your Spirit that continually guides us, reminding us of all you have taught us. Make us faithful as we respond to your invitation to follow you.

THURSDAY

AM *Psalms: 70, 71*

PM *Psalm: 74*

Genesis 42:29–38

Mark 4:21–34

1 Corinthians 6:12–20

As children, we often daydream about the day when no one will tell us what to do. We can eat what we want, stay up as late as we want, do whatever we want. When adulthood arrives, we realize quickly that these choices have consequences—ill-fitting clothes and exhaustion, to name a couple.

In today's epistle text, Paul writes to the church about freedom. Immersed as they are in philosophical systems that run contrary to the gospel, the people of God are wrestling with what it looks like to be followers of Jesus. Paul affirms a popular notion of the day: *All things are lawful for me.* However, he adds two caveats: not all things are beneficial, nor should we be dominated by anything. Paul seeks to avoid two extremes: legalism and antinomianism (lawlessness). He rejects the notion that followers of Christ are found righteous by the external indicators formerly considered evidence of one's righteousness. However, he also rejects the suggestion that this freedom from the law can be equated to a "live and let live" way of being. This hollow understanding of freedom is merely slavery to a new master: the self and its desires.

A life of faithfulness cannot be rooted in the hard, unbreachable boundaries of legalism, nor can it be found in the false freedom of lawlessness. In fact, a life of faithfulness cannot be rooted in any moral system because faithfulness is not about morality but about identity. The question is never, what's the right choice? The question is always, who am I? The question held for the church in Corinth, and it holds for us today. Who are we? When we have found our true home in the family of God and placed our full weight in our belovedness as children of God, we begin to see how that identity informs the choices we make. Our identity invites us to live into the family resemblance. Who we are shapes what we do.

To demonstrate his point, Paul takes on the issue of sexual ethics. Why do we eschew indulgent, self-gratifying sexual encounters outside the covenant of marriage? Because we are bound by the law? No. We abstain because God raised Jesus from the dead, declaring that what happens to our bodies (and what we do *with* our bodies) matters. What God has done in and for Jesus, God will do in and for us. We are resurrection people. The same Spirit that raised our Lord from the dead is alive and at work in us now. Therefore, we honor God with our bodies.

It is not the morality checklist many of us crave, nor is it a free pass to live in the false freedom of our desires. What we are given is far better: an invitation to lean into our identity as children of God and co-heirs with Christ and to wrestle with the question, how does who I am shape what I do? It's not about mastering morality but submitting to and embracing an identity.

—SDL

REFLECTION & PRACTICE

01 In some Christian traditions the message to ourselves and others is that the objective of being a Christian is to "be good." Paul's admonition to the church in Corinth, however, is founded on this: "You are not your own . . . honor God with your bodies" (1 Corinthians 6:19, 20).

- How does this change the way we relate to one another? In our home, in our neighborhood, in our work?
- How might we teach this to our children and our young people?

02 Paul says that our bodies are members of Christ himself.
- How does this inform us regarding our relationships with others in the church?
- What would it take for you and your local church to demonstrate what Paul is saying to the church in Corinth?

03 Paul says that when we are united with the Lord we are one with him in spirit.
- What does it mean to be united with the Lord? How does that change our identity?
- Does Paul infer that our conduct no longer matters? If the rules are no longer the guideline for our conduct, what is our guide? What difference will that make in our living with one another?

PRAYER

Lord, our lives are so often driven by our efforts to "find ourselves." But it is in you that we finally know who we are, why we live, and how we may love others as we love ourselves. Thank you for providing such transformation that the source of our living, the source of our being, the foundation of our identity is found in your love for us. Your Spirit's presence gives us the power and the motivation to honor you. Thank you for the freedom and the joy we find when we honor you in all we do.

FRIDAY

AM *Psalm: 69*

PM *Psalm: 73*

Genesis 43:1–15

Mark 4:35–41

1 Corinthians 7:1–9

Lent is not for the faint of heart! It is a challenging journey. We confront our complacency, examine our hearts, and ask probing questions of ourselves and of those who journey with us. One of the most challenging questions we should ask is this: Do we really know who Jesus is?

In today's Gospel passage is an account of one of the many times Jesus crossed the Sea of Galilee. Jesus has been teaching the people who have gathered around him. He's told them stories, using parables to illustrate the kingdom of God. Whenever he is alone with the disciples he explains the parables. The disciples are getting to know Jesus better and better. On this day, when evening comes, he instructs them to get in a boat with him to cross to the other side of the lake. As they cross, a furious storm develops. The boat is tossed by the wind, and waves crash into the boat, nearly swamping it. The disciples are terrified! Jesus, exhausted from the constant pressure of the crowds, is asleep in the stern. In their fear they wake Jesus, crying, "Teacher, don't you care if we drown?" (Mark 4:38).

Jesus stands up and speaks to the wind and the waves, and the lake becomes calm. Mark tells us they are now even more terrified. "Who is this? Even the wind and the waves obey him!" (Mark 4:41).

We must be very careful that we do not diminish the terror in this experience. To simply suggest that we should take heart when we face trials because Jesus is with us misses the point. Sometimes terrifying things occur even when Jesus is with us—a searing loss, a frightening diagnosis, a natural disaster, a gut-wrenching betrayal. Sometimes, if we are honest, our trust is tested to the ultimate limits.

The Lenten journey is intended to open our hearts and minds to a new grasp of the identity of Jesus of Nazareth. We dare not tame him to the point that there is little to no scandal in what happened during Holy Week. The disciples think they know him. They have been walking with him, listening to him, and watching as he heals the sick and delivers the demon-possessed. And now winds and waves meekly obey him, and they are terrified!

Are you willing to *really* get to know Jesus? It could be dangerous!

—SDL

REFLECTION & PRACTICE

01 The behavior of Jesus during the storm has lost its shock value for us because church history came to know and believe that Jesus was both human and divine. This aspect of Jesus's identity was not at all clear to the disciples at this stage in their own discipleship. They did not understand that Jesus was making God known to them through every word and deed.

- We are comfortable with the information that Jesus is one with God, but what would it mean to take seriously that everything Jesus said or did revealed God's self to us?

- Try reading through the entirety of Mark in a single sitting this week. (As the shortest Gospel, it shouldn't take long.) When Jesus speaks or acts, pause and remind yourself: this is who God is. How might this practice reorient our understanding of God away from an idol created in our own image to a more faithful understanding of the heart and mission of God?

02 This story strips away any notion of Jesus as merely a kind, insightful healer, sent to apply a Band-Aid to our wounds and sins while we await eternity. He is God in the flesh, full of power and might, taking on the chaos wrought by sin and death at work in creation.

- Where have you witnessed God's chaos-confronting power in your life?
- As commissioned followers of Jesus, what might it look like to partner with God in confronting the powers of chaos at work in the world? How can you be an agent of reconciliation, peace, and healing in the relationships and systems in your life?
- Sometimes God rightly orders chaos this side of eternity; other times we must wait in the tension of unresolved brokenness until the day of Christ's return. How do we wait in hope for destruction of chaos itself?

PRAYER

Lord, thank you for revealing God the Father to us. Unsettle all the false and idolatrous beliefs we have about who God is and send your Spirit to remind us that in you, we know God. Thank you for confronting the powers of chaos at work around us. Empower us to trust you with what remains unresolved this side of eternity, and make clear to us the ways by which we might be agents of peace, reconciliation, and restoration.

SATURDAY

AM *Psalms: 75, 76*

PM *Psalms: 23, 27*

Genesis 43:16–34

Mark 5:1–20

1 Corinthians 7:10–24

Mangled chains. Shattered shackles. A man, naked and covered with self-inflicted wounds, prowls among the tombs. Without warning, he screams into the abyss at forces no one else can see. He is the living dead, unnamed, ostracized, alone. He is at home nowhere, not even in his own mind or body.

This is the scene that greets Jesus on the shore of the region of the Gerasenes—gentile territory. Jesus and his disciples have just crossed the Sea of Galilee, and it was not an ordinary crossing. A storm accosted them halfway, making their demise certain until Jesus stood and commanded the wind and waves: *Peace! Be still.* The sea obeyed, submitting to the Lord of creation incarnate. Now Jesus faces chaos in a new form. Instead of tumultuous waves and whipping winds, a storm is raging inside the man who is now running toward and falling at Jesus's feet. Jesus and the legion of demons within the man do battle. It is not a conflict between equal but opposing forces. The legion declares Jesus to be the Son of the Most High God, and begs his permission to flee into a herd of swine. Jesus assents, and the demons leave the man, who is now free but bears on his body the marks of the chaos wrought upon him.

The crowds gather, mouths agape. A herd of pigs rests at the bottom of the sea, and a man who is well known for terrorizing his community sits dressed, calm, and still. Instead of rejoicing at this miracle performed among them, their hearts are filled with fear. Who is this man—this Jewish man—infringing on their territory, interfering in their lives? They prefer the chaos they recognize to the power they do not.

The freed man, however, feels differently. The wounds on his body as well as the experiences seared into his mind of being chained, isolated, and afraid serve as reminders of what once was. He knows intimately the power of the chaotic darkness. Now, in the eyes of this Jewish rabbi, he sees light. Where once he saw nothing but disorder, confusion, and pain, he now sees a hope-filled future. He has made his choice, and his choice is Jesus.

Jesus has already chosen his twelve Jewish disciples—the representation of the tribes of Israel. But that does not mean there is no role for this gentile man to fill. Jesus commissions the man to testify to what the Lord has done for him throughout the gentile Decapolis. While the fullness of God's mission has yet to come to all people, it begins here, on the banks of the sea with a man formerly possessed by the enemy—bruised and broken externally but healed and whole within.

Jesus is making himself known through words of power and deeds of might. Chaos crumbles at his voice. Disorder dissipates, revealing newly ordered lives and hearts. God is doing something altogether new. Will we rejoice, repent, and follow, or will we turn away in fear?

—JCM

REFLECTION & PRACTICE

01 This story is filled with implications regarding the identity of Jesus. He has just calmed a storm on the lake. Now, in gentile territory, he faces a storm on the shore in the form of a man possessed by demons. Mark continues to reveal that the disciples, beginning to realize that Jesus just may be the Messiah, are still confused as to what that means.

- What does this story intend to reveal about the identity of Jesus?
- Why is it significant that Jesus is seen in gentile territory when this event occurs?

02 The demons call themselves "Legion." That may mean one thousand (Roman legions usually comprised one thousand soldiers).

- What does the name imply in regard to Jesus's sovereignty over all things?
- How might this event further inform the disciples about the nature of Jesus's ministry as Messiah?

03 Religious tradition in Judaism expected Jews to avoid contaminating their holiness by associating with anything that was unholy. In this case, the depths of unholiness were demonstrated in the demon-possessed man.

- What was the impact of this man's unholiness on the holiness of Jesus? Where did the holiness of Jesus reside?
- What do Jesus's actions in this story say about our duty as followers of Jesus in a world so often characterized by ugliness, brokenness, and despair?

04 In this case, Jesus did not demand that the man, now cleansed and whole, keep silent. He was told to tell the whole region how much Jesus had done for him.

- Why do you think Jesus did not allow him to accompany him back to Galilee?
- What does Jesus's instruction imply about the ministry of Jesus? What does it imply about our ministry?

PRAYER

Thank you, Lord, for your gracious compassion toward the broken man in this story. Thank you for the hope it gives us for how you wish to work in our lives and in the lives of those around us—those we know and love, and those who frighten or threaten us. As we walk this journey, help us to recognize our desperate need of your compassion and grace. May we come to realize again that there is no storm, no evil, no level of brokenness that exceeds your capacity to bring hope, healing, and restoration.

THIRD SUNDAY IN LENT

AM *Psalms: 93, 96*

PM *Psalm: 34*

Genesis 44:1–17

John 5:25–29

Romans 8:1–10

It is Sunday, and respite from the rigor of fasting and self-denial, or of investment in serving others as a Lenten discipline, is welcomed. Praise should be the refrain of the day. The psalmist captures that sense of praise and thanksgiving: "Let all creation rejoice before the Lord, for he comes, he comes to judge the earth. He will judge the world in righteousness and the peoples in his faithfulness" (96:13).

There is no fear in this judgment. This is a God who brings salvation! The apostle Paul said, "Therefore, there is now no condemnation for those who are in Christ Jesus, because through Christ Jesus the law of the Spirit who gives life has set you free from the law of sin and death" (Romans 8:1–2).

Worship is not a one-way street. In worship we encounter the speaking God. In contrast to the idols that so often captured the attention of Israel, gods who were deaf and dumb, the God of Israel, the Creator of the ends of the earth, is a speaking God. He addresses the people of the earth.

In our Gospel lesson for today, Jesus declares that the time has come when the dead—those spiritually dead because of sin and alienation from God—"will hear the voice of the Son of God and those who hear will live" (John 5:25). In worship we celebrate that voice. It is life-giving, transforming all who hear, providing life, hope, restoration, forgiveness, cleansing. And that spiritual resurrection Jesus declares serves as a foretaste of the final resurrection when, like Christ, we shall be raised to new life with God. Because he has entered into creation as Son of Man, taking on our humanity in all its dimensions, he has the authority to speak life into us.

The religious leaders of Jesus's day are furious. In their minds, he is a pretender to the throne. They cannot conceive of the reality that stands before them. Their judgments are harsh, condemning, and divisive. They insist that they know authority when they see it—and Jesus, they are sure, does not have it! Their assessment does not alter reality. Jesus, the Son of God, has authority that they know nothing about, cannot exercise, and cannot hinder. This is the One who spoke worlds into existence, who sends demons fleeing in terror, who heals the sick, straightens crooked limbs, gives sight to the blind, and even raises the dead.

In the midst of your Lenten journey, on this Sunday, lift up your head! Breathe the breath of God. Listen carefully for the voice. Sing praises. The One who gives life is here! Praise him!

—JCM

REFLECTION & PRACTICE

01 Every Sunday, even during the Lenten season, is a resurrection day in which we declare what is called the mystery of our faith: Christ has died, Christ has risen, Christ will come again.

- How might you intentionally approach worship today in a spirit of celebration for what God has done and will do?

02 God has chosen to make God's self known to us. We not only have
the testimony of the Gospels bearing witness to the life of Christ, but
we also have the presence of the Spirit, who guides and teaches us.

- As a spiritual discipline, with a spirit of thanksgiving recall
how you have experienced the voice of God in the past.

03 We celebrate the ways God has spoken in the past, yet we do not
always rely upon them to fuel a vibrant, current faith today. How is
God speaking to you *today*? Unquestionably, there are times when
God is silent, but sometimes we have not given ourselves over to the
practice of patient listening. How might you create space for that
patient listening?

04 Brother Lawrence, a monk in the 1600s, devoted his life to practicing
the presence of God even during the most mundane of tasks. He
described a practice of attentiveness in which he trained himself to
be constantly in tune and conversation with God.

- How might we engage in the prayer practice of attention in
our own lives?
- What habits, relationships, or devotions might need to be
reexamined in order to create space for such a practice?

PRAYER

*Lord, we are grateful that you are not a God unknown, that instead you
have revealed yourself through the Word, the Spirit, and the church. The
more we come to know you, the more deeply we love you. We confess that
at times we have approached worship as a one-way conversation. With
mouths busy speaking, our ears cannot listen. Forgive our inattentiveness
to your voice. Teach us to listen well on this day devoted to worship, and
every day.*

MONDAY

AM *Psalm: 80*

PM *Psalms: 77, 79*

Genesis 44:18–34

Mark 5:21–43

1 Corinthians 7:25–31

Desperation is the enemy of inhibition. When you are desperate, you do things you might never dream of doing otherwise. A synagogue leader like the one in our Gospel passage for today would not likely bow at anyone else's feet. As a community leader and a religious authority, you live with a certain decorum that is expected. But this man is desperate. His young daughter is dying. Nothing else matters in a moment like that!

A woman hemorrhaging blood is an outcast. Were she in Jerusalem, she would be ineligible to enter the temple. It is likely that the local synagogue is off limits to her as well. Every normal activity necessary to survival is hindered by her growing weakness and social rejection. All her resources are gone. She is desperate.

Mark's stories in this passage are a graphic illustration of what Jesus means in yesterday's reading from John 5 about the dead hearing the voice of God and living. We don't know how they know, but these two people are convinced that the only hope they have is Jesus. The crowd is large, pressing in on Jesus and his disciples, but two people are so determined to reach him that, whatever it takes, whatever they have to face, they are going to get to Jesus.

Jairus doesn't care who sees him. He prostrates himself at the feet of Jesus in desperation, pleading with Jesus to come and heal his daughter. The woman, desperately afraid of being found out and trying to draw as little attention as possible, wants to just touch his clothes. She believes that little amount of contact will be enough to heal her.

These two have heard his voice. In spite of the noise, the press of the crowd, and the demands being made by so many others, these two heard the Voice. It beckoned to them. It offered life to them. In their desperation, they have found hope.

Somehow, in the press of our busy schedules, crowded lives, and quiet desperation, this Lenten journey could well be the time when we tune our hearts to hear the Voice. We do not have to coerce the Voice. He is speaking. He is always speaking. It is in this journey, as we work our way toward the cross and resurrection, that we just may hear the Voice at levels we have never known before. Get desperate enough to find the quiet space to listen. He is speaking.

—JCM

REFLECTION & PRACTICE

01 Both Jairus and the bleeding woman took a risk. Jairus risked shame and slander for falling at the feet of this controversial teacher. The woman risked ridicule and abuse for defiling the teacher with her unclean hands. Their desperate need overwhelmed any social mores that previously would have held them back.

- What social expectations might prevent you from falling at the feet of Jesus and asking him for what you need?
- If nothing held you back—neither pride nor social pressure— what would you ask of the Lord?

02 Though Jesus was the agent of healing, both the fear-stricken father and the bleeding woman cooperated in the healing they experienced. The man approached Jesus. The woman reached out for his cloak.

Jesus met them in their reaching and drew them forward into a new, transformed future.

- As believers living in light of the resurrection and Pentecost, our reaching out is empowered, even *enabled*, by the Spirit. What might it look like for us, empowered by the Holy Spirit, to reach out for Christ in search of healing, in trust that he will meet us in the reach?

03 In a sense, Jesus raised both the woman and the girl to new life. Both responded to the healing voice of Jesus, inviting them into resurrected life.

- How have you experienced death, whether literal or metaphorical?
- How might the voice of Jesus be inviting you into resurrected life? Ask the Holy Spirit to breathe the breath of life into what feels dead in you.

PRAYER

Lord, how deeply we need you. We need your healing touch. We need your resurrecting power. We need your voice of love to break through our clogged ears and soften our hardened hearts. Yet, even in our need, our pride prevents us from falling at your feet. Our concern for appearances keeps us on our feet, arms crossed and hearts closed. Send your Spirit to awaken us to your voice of love. Give us the courage to reach for you. You have already reached for us.

TUESDAY

AM *Psalm: 78:1–39*

PM *Psalm: 78:40–72*

Genesis 45:1–15

Mark 6:1–13

1 Corinthians 7:32–40

It is easy to be blinded by familiarity. Some psychologists speak of "boundary states." When you enter a room for the first time, you will normally see more of the room than you will ever see again. The more you are in and out of the room the less you will see. A burned-out light bulb, accumulating clutter, dust, or smudges on the wall or door have become so familiar that you cease to notice them. When someone else enters the room for the first time they will more readily see those features than you.

In Nazareth, they know Jesus. They saw him grow up. They know his family. There is no reason to expect a boy from Nazareth to be special in any extraordinary way. It is one thing to be one of the neighborhood's "good" boys. It is something else altogether to speak with wisdom or authority beyond the rest of us!

69

For many, this is the season of Lent, *again*. We have been here before. The scriptures are familiar, and the devotional thoughts suggest that we once again embark on the Lenten journey. We should humble ourselves and look deeply at our spiritual lives. We should approach Holy Week in a way that will make the celebration of Easter and the resurrection come alive with a new zeal and passion. But there is a danger here. It is that we are here, *again*.

We engage in prayer, fasting, and service to others in Jesus's name as part of our Lenten routine, as simply the way we live in this season. But what might the Spirit be saying to you this year that you were not ready to hear in the past? What fresh insight into a Scripture passage might nudge your heart and mind toward a new dimension of spiritual growth and maturity? What new habits might the Spirit prompt you to adopt in your walk with Christ? What habits—even good ones—have become so routine that you can and often do engage in them mindlessly? Another question might be, "Are we allowing growth in others that God is prompting in them?"

My wife, Susan, and I celebrated our 55th wedding anniversary in 2019. I know her well. By this time, we are both rather predictable. But as we participated in our Lenten journey, I found myself a bit unsettled by her new insights into Scripture and the spiritual disciplines we engaged in. It became liberating for both of us for me to say, "I have never seen that before. Thank you for your insight. Thank you for challenging me."

Don't be blinded by your holy routine. Maybe, just maybe, there is something new to learn.

—JCM

REFLECTION & PRACTICE

01 Think back to when you first came to know the Lord. Or, if you came to know the Lord at a very young age, think back to when your faith came alive for the first time.

- What captured your attention as you awakened to God's hand at work in and around you? What did you notice or learn about yourself, the world, or God that you had never experienced before?

- Could it be that clutter or dust might have accumulated in our hearts or lives without our even realizing it? How can Lent give us new eyes to see what has gone unnoticed?

02 Those of us who have followed Jesus for a long time often look down upon new followers of Jesus who are full of enthusiasm, vigor, and passion. While there is a great deal to be said about ordinary, long-suffering obedience, could our condescension be born not of wisdom but of cynicism?

- What does cynicism look like in people of faith? Could cynicism be lurking in the shadowy corners of your heart?
- Does cynicism require forgiveness or healing? Invite the Spirit to guide you in this reflection.

03 After his rejection at Nazareth, Jesus commissions his disciples to do the work of the kingdom in the surrounding villages. And if the people reject them? Move along. They are not ready to listen and obey.

- God is continually inviting us to receive and enact God's kingdom. However, persistent no's to God's invitation will have consequences: hardened hearts and ears less in tune with the voice of the Spirit. How is your hearing? Does the voice of the Lord seem faint? Silence from the Lord is not necessarily indicative of a hardened heart, but it is appropriate to, as John Wesley says, "examine our own hearts before God."
- When we say yes to God, we experience the blessing of bearing witness to God's work in and among us. When has your yes to God allowed you to see kingdom transformation in yourself or others?

PRAYER

Lord, we confess that our hearts often grow cold and hard. Cynicism and even bitterness creep into our spirits, blinding us to the movement of your Spirit in and among us. Forgive us when we are passive in our faith, even negligent. Stir the flames of the love we once knew—not into the quickly extinguished flash of passion of untested faith but into the rich, long-lasting burn that warms all who gather near.

WEDNESDAY

AM *Psalm: 119:97–120*

PM *Psalms: 81, 82*

Genesis 45:16–28

Mark 6:13–29

1 Corinthians 8:1–13

What are we willing to give up for love? In 1936, a king gave up his crown for love. My great-grandmother gave up her citizenship to marry my great-grandfather (the law of the land at the time.) Parents give up a tidy home for love of their children's messy, crazy, joy-filled playing. I daily give up half my breakfast to my toddler, who always seems to want what I'm having.

In today's epistle text, Paul addresses an issue that feels very distant from us: eating meat that has been offered to idols. On the surface, this seems like a contextual issue that has very little to do with contemporary faith. On the contrary, the challenge of this text is very timely. The church in Corinth is wrestling with how to handle meat, most of which has been offered to idols prior to coming to market. One segment of the church, comfortable in their freedom in Christ, takes no issue with consuming such meat because they know idols are worthless, false gods. Others in the church feel differently. Perhaps they are new believers or were at one time deeply entrenched in the pagan practices of the surrounding culture. They now follow Christ and desire a clean break from the pagan practices of the past, including consuming meat offered to idols.

The Corinthian church is at an impasse. There seems to be no way forward. Should they compromise—perhaps institute a Meatless Monday fellowship and a Thursday BBQ? What does faithful Christian community look like in such a case? While our congregations today might not be wrestling over meat in quite this way, a multitude of other divisive issues almost certainly come to mind quickly. We find ourselves asking, "What's the right answer?" But a more fruitful question might be, "Who are we as the people of God?" How we answer that question informs our response to the meat (and any other) dilemmas.

As the body of Christ, we are those who are called to embody together the self-giving, self-pouring-out love of Jesus. If we truly call ourselves the body of Christ—referencing a body that was crucified—then our life together must be cross-shaped. Our rights, our preferences, our desires—even our knowledge—must submit to love for the sake of the other. When we refuse to submit to one another out of reverence for Christ, whom (or what) are we truly worshiping?

If insisting upon our rights is indicative of false worship, what is true worship? Paul once again directs us, this time to the *Shema*—but the *Shema* reimagined in light of Christ. True worship is to love the Lord our God with our heart, soul, mind, and strength *and* to love our neighbor as ourselves, as Christ has loved us. This cross-shaped love outplays knowledge every time. As we live together as Jesus followers, if we must choose between being loving and being right, let us be loving. Cross-shaped, self-emptying love will be our faithful guide.

—*SDL*

REFLECTION & PRACTICE

01 The Corinthian church was at an impasse. The tension was high, and it is likely that each side felt justified in holding firmly to their conviction. It is not unusual for local churches to have to wrestle with issues that could potentially divide the community of faith.

- Have you been part of a church that has been at an impasse over an issue? How did it affect you? How did it impact the relationships in the church? How did it affect the worship experience of the church?
- What measures were taken to address the impasse? How were the ways the church approached the issues different from how they might have been in another setting? In what ways could the approach have been more shaped by the gospel of Jesus?

02 Every local church is made up of people at various stages in their spiritual journey. In the Corinthian church, it appears that the mature believers were being challenged by Paul to give up some of their previously held convictions.
- How does our response to conflict reflect our love for one another?
- Does spiritual maturity give us more rights than another?

03 Paul says that to exercise our rights can become a stumbling block, that to violate the conscience of a less mature or less long-standing member of the body of Christ is to sin against Christ.
- How may we avoid becoming prideful in our dealing with others who are struggling to grow in their walk with Christ?
- What can we do to contribute to the flourishing of those whose faith is new and whose journey is still being formed?

PRAYER

Father, your church, the bride of Christ, matters deeply you. Yet we live in a world often characterized by the assertion of our rights. We confess that sometimes in our determination to be free to shape our life journeys as we choose, we can overlook the impact of our choices on those around us. Help us to live in such surrender to you that our relationships within your church are formed by our love for your Son and for your church. May those with whom we worship find in us a deep and self-giving love, even when it means a surrender of our perceived rights.

THURSDAY

AM *Psalms: 42, 43*

PM *Psalms: 85, 86*

Genesis 46:1–7, 28–34

Mark 6:30–46

1 Corinthians 9:1–15

Sometimes the Lord gives us an opportunity, and we are blinded by our lack of imagination.

The Twelve, the disciples of Jesus, have just returned from the mission on which he sent them. It must have been an exhilarating experience! "They went out and preached that people should repent. They drove out many demons and anointed many sick people with oil and healed them" (Mark 6:12–13). Things happened! What they had seen Jesus do, they were able to do, and their effective service attracted attention.

As they are reporting to Jesus what they did and taught, crowds gather, pressing in on them, likely clamoring for more of what the apostles have been doing for them. They are exhausted, hungry, and overwhelmed, so Jesus invites them to come away with him to rest and replenish. Getting back into a boat, they head to "a solitary place" (v. 32).

But the crowds, seeing where they are headed, run on foot and get there first. By the time the boat arrives, the crowd is already gathered.

Here we see an amazing contrast between the compassion of Jesus and the pragmatism of the apostles. These sent ones are appropriately concerned for the people who have gathered in this "remote place" (v. 35). It is late in the day, and the people need to eat. "Send the people away," they say. "They need to eat."

"You give them something to eat," says Jesus (v. 37).

These apostles have just been reporting to Jesus what they've done. People were delivered from demons. Others were healed. Now their first response is, "We can't do that!"

Here they are, pressed upon by the crowds that have come to them because of what they have done, and their imaginations fail. Jesus has given them "authority over impure spirits" (v. 7). People were healed of diseases. And now, in the face of human hunger, they are powerless to see beyond their own meager resources.

Compassion for "sheep without a shepherd" (v. 34) is admirable. Having concern for the welfare of the needy around us is appropriate. Assessing our own resources to meet needs is wise. But, at some level, the journey of faith requires that we realize where our true resources lie. What if the apostles would say to one another, "We have seen demons flee. We have seen disease defeated. What is human hunger in contrast to that? Let's throw our lives into however Jesus chooses to demonstrate his kingdom."

Jesus and the apostles have been preaching about the kingdom of God. In their mission they have already become demonstrations of the kingdom. What might happen if the apostles could imagine a kingdom-of-God response to this massive need? How might their faith be transformed if they allow their prior experience with God's provision to open their imaginations to the possibilities inherent in this new circumstance?

Are we invested enough in God's kingdom to see beyond our resources to the resources of the One who has sent us? It takes a sanctified imagination to see kingdom answers to staggering need. But if this kingdom is real, God just may be up to something—and we could be part of it!

—JCM

REFLECTION & PRACTICE

01 Doubtless we have all been overwhelmed by the needs of others—
needs that often seem insatiable. Sometimes we respond through
disengagement and distance, overwhelmed and frustrated by our
inability to meet a need. Other times we frantically hustle and work
to find a solution out of the resources we can cobble together.

- Both responses are born from the idolatrous assumption that
we are the source. What would happen if we remembered
and practiced the truth that we are *partners* in redemption
and provision, not the source? How would this change our
posture toward the need we encounter and also toward those
with needs?

02 A sanctified imagination is one that is shaped by the character of
God as faithful and trustworthy. It gives our mind the wiggle room
it needs to escape the chains of scarcity and fear.

- Life experience, trauma, and even personality make us sus-
ceptible to the voices of scarcity and fear in different ways.
Where are you most vulnerable to these voices? How might
God want to heal these wounds?
- God is always the agent of sanctification in us—including the
sanctification of our imaginations—but what practices might
we incorporate into our lives to give God space to dream
God's dreams in us?

PRAYER

*Lord, you are not limited by our shallow imaginations. You are not bound
by the boundaries our minds try to impose upon you. Thank you for
inviting us to join you in the kingdom work of redemption, provision, and
healing, even though we often resist out of fear. Loose our imaginations,
Lord. Sanctify them holy, that we might catch a glimpse of what you desire
to do in, through, and among us.*

FRIDAY

AM *Psalm: 88*

PM *Psalms: 91, 92*

Genesis 47:1–26

Mark 6:47–56

1 Corinthians 9:16–27

Sometimes the Lenten journey takes us into uncomfortable territory. At some points it can become unsettling, especially if we have lived with a myth of certainty. The Christian journey does not promise the kind of certainty we sometimes crave and even claim. Even as we try our best to know and trust Christ, what we are going through can reveal, sometimes painfully, our basic uncertainty about some of the things we thought we knew about ourselves and about God. Our interactions with others under stress or in conflict can be difficult. A devastating diagnosis of disease in ourselves or a loved one can shake us to the core. When our most passionate and fervent prayers go unanswered, we are often disillusioned.

Then we come to a passage that appears in three of the four Gospels in which Jesus walks on the water. Many of us are not sure what to do with the story. It is not lost on us that we are in Lent and are headed toward the crucifixion. And we know that the reason we take this journey is that there is an Easter celebration ahead of us. The One who was crucified, dead, and buried is raised! Resurrection occurs! So, we reason, if we can believe in the resurrection, what is the problem with a little walking on water? Jesus walking on the water does not resolve confusion among the disciples either. In the story of his calming the seas in Mark 4, their terror in the face of the ferocious storm is surpassed by their terror that the storm subsided at his command. Now, according to Mark, seeing Jesus walking on the water at first "terrified" and then "completely amazed" them (6:50, 51). "They had not understood about the loaves," Mark writes; "their hearts were hardened" (v. 52).

Mark intends to draw us deeper and deeper into the realization that Jesus is more than a teacher, a rabbi, or a healer. While those who walk with him think they know him, somehow they continue to miss what is going on as he makes his way toward Jerusalem.

In all three accounts of Jesus walking on the water, he identifies himself to the disciples with the words "I AM." In the Gospel of John are the seven "I AM" sayings of Jesus, so filled with meaning and so intentional in identifying Jesus with God's self-revelation in Exodus: "I AM . . . This is my name forever, the name you shall call me from generation to generation" (Exodus 3:14a, 15b). Here, in a profound moment of self-revelation, Jesus identifies himself to his disciples—and they miss it!

We sometimes miss it too. We waver. We fear. We are often terribly uncertain. Perhaps we need to listen better than the disciples. Our certainty dare not be in ourselves. He is our certainty. He is the "I AM."

—JCM

REFLECTION & PRACTICE

01 The myth of certainty suggests that it is possible to be free from doubt, misunderstandings, and ambiguity. The church has sometimes propagated this myth through social pressure, suggesting that those with questions are unfaithful and unworthy.

- What is the appeal of certainty, even when we know it is an empty promise?
- Why do we fear uncertainty?

02 God often meets with us in unexpected ways when we finally surrender the need for uncertainty.

- Have you found this to be true? How did this transform your relationship with God?
- How might sharing our experience of the unraveling of certainty and God's faithfulness in the midst of that edify the church?

03 When we have made an idol of certainty, our hearts become hardened. We are unable to perceive what God is doing in our midst because of our expectations.

- What might be some indicators that our hearts have become hard?
- What would it look like to surrender the idol of certainty and allow the Spirit to soften any hardness of heart in you?

04 Christ is our certainty.

- How does this truth differ from the myth of certainty that attempts to guarantee outcomes and experiences?
- How might we come to know God in a transformative way if we rooted our faith in God's eternally certain presence?

PRAYER

Lord, we confess that at times we have served the false god of certainty instead of you. We are afraid and full of doubt and so cling to anything that feels solid. Forgive us. You do not call us to flawless faith, without question or doubt. You call us to lean into you and your persistent presence, regardless of circumstances or outcome. Soften our hardened hearts, that we might see you at work among us and join you there.

SATURDAY

AM *Psalms: 87, 90*

PM *Psalm: 136*

Genesis 47:27–48:7

Mark 7:1–23

1 Corinthians 10:1–13

The New Testament Pharisees get a bad rap. They easily become the scapegoat for what we believe to be hypocritical and legalistic religiosity. But what was remarkable about the Pharisees was their genuine zeal to demonstrate the call to holiness for the people of God. They were not jealous of Jesus because he had great crowds following him. Their genuine fear was that Jesus appeared antagonistic toward the law of God as they understood it. The Pharisees loved the law. For them it was a demonstration of the holiness of God, a reflection of the perfect mind of God.

Pharisees were the Holiness tradition of Judaism. They longed to see a recovery of holiness in the everyday lives of the people. They wanted to be sure that they and those to whom they ministered were aware of what observance of the law required. In Judaism over the centuries, hundreds of regulations were developed for everyday life. This is what the Pharisees mean when they refer to "the tradition of the elders" in

Mark 7:5. These regulations covered nearly every conceivable activity of life, including, for instance, rules about how one was to eat. Eating with unwashed hands was a violation that defiled the eater.

No list of descriptions or requirements will ever be enough. Eventually, the rules become the focus, the law becomes a deity, and life is bound in endless measurements of what is holy. But before we criticize the Pharisees who were resisting Jesus, perhaps we ought to look more closely at how easy it is for us to elevate external markers of holiness to the level of Scripture-like authority. We are tempted to measure the religious credibility of other people by a certain set of markers that we have learned or adopted for ourselves. Those markers, often intended to give guidance to the young or immature, can become an end in themselves.

The law can become disembodied and idolatrous when we forget that we are supposed to worship the Giver of the law, not the law itself. That we worship God is best demonstrated by the integrity of our relationships, our love for God, and our love for our fellow human beings. And that must flow from within us. If what is within us readily corresponds with what is vile, vulgar, and broken in the culture around us, we demonstrate the truth of the words of Jesus: "What comes out of a person is what defiles them. For it is from within, out of a person's heart, that evil thoughts come" (Mark 7:20–21a).

In this journey with Jesus toward the cross, as we examine the Lenten passages, are we willing to allow those passages to examine us? Jesus did not come to impose additional laws, rules, and guidelines. He came to provide the means by which our hearts can be changed. The center from which we live may be so altered by his grace and mercy that we live a holy transparency that flows from deep within us. Jesus called that a "river of living water" (John 7:38). Flow, river! Flow!

—JCM

REFLECTION & PRACTICE

01 The Pharisees were afraid that Jesus would lead the people of God astray through what they perceived as his disregard for the law.

- How does our own fear for the church tempt us toward legalism?
- Is it possible to have the best intentions and still find yourself working against what the Lord is doing?

02 Many Pharisees were of the belief that if only the people of God would be faithful to the law as a unified group for a moment in time, the Messiah would come and restore all things.

- What is the danger in believing God's action in the world is contingent upon our righteousness?
- In what ways is it possible that we affirm a similar belief in our lives today—that God's favor rests upon our righteousness?

03 The Pharisees measured the holiness of the people of God through external markers like ritual washings, food laws, and holy days.

- What are some of the external markers we use, consciously or unconsciously, to measure the holiness of others?
- How do we discern the difference between Christian account ability and unholy judgment?

04 Our faith is best exemplified in the integrity of our relationships with God and with one another. Our relationship with God cannot be separated from our relationship with others. The former informs and shapes the latter.

- How has your relationship with God transformed your relationship with other people?
- When a spirit of unforgiveness or an inclination toward merciless judgment arises in us, how might we attend to the source of these attitudes, instead of merely managing our behavior? What would it look like to lean into the Holy Spirit more deeply, inviting the Spirit to reveal, forgive, and heal these attitudes?

PRAYER

Lord, we love you and long to be faithful to your call to holy living. We confess that, in our zeal and desire for control, we often settle for external markers of holiness instead of seeking after true holiness: a transformed heart marked by embodied love for you and others. Forgive us for the ways in which we have wounded others with unholy judgment, forgetting that you alone see and know the human heart. Reshape our hearts and minds, that we might more perfectly love you and that our love might overflow in our relationships with others.

FOURTH SUNDAY IN LENT

AM *Psalms: 66, 67*

PM *Psalms: 19, 46*

Genesis 18:8–22

John 6:27–40

Romans 8:11–25

For many Christians, our spiritual lives are characterized by vague generalities. We believe in God, but we have little to no understanding of God's nature or character. We testify to being followers of Jesus, but we have very little awareness of the purposes for which he took on human flesh. We know he lived and taught in the Middle East and was crucified on a Roman cross. We celebrate Easter, but we cannot explain the significance of the resurrection to our faith.

The Gospel of John, from which our devotional is drawn for today's reading, was written with a very specific purpose: "But these are written that you may believe that Jesus is the Messiah, the Son of God, and that by believing you may have life in his name" (John 20:31). The writer of the Gospel crafted the story with skill, insight, and intentionality. At every opportunity he urges the reader to recognize who Jesus was.

In today's reading—one of the seven "I AM" sayings of Jesus found in the Gospel of John—there is a piercing and overarching theme throughout the passage. Earlier in chapter 6, Jesus took five small barley loaves and two small fish from a young boy's lunch. He gave thanks to the Father, broke the loaves and fish, and fed five thousand men, with thousands more when women and children were included in the count. It so impressed the crowd that they intended to make Jesus king by force. Food for everyone, whenever you wanted or needed it? What was the downside of that? Jesus would have none of it, so he withdrew to a solitary place to pray.

Today's passage recounts what happens the next day when the crowds find him. They gather around him in eager anticipation that they could be fed again. But Jesus says to them, "You are here because of the loaves and the fish, but you do not understand who I am." They want him to give them bread and fish. He wants to give them himself. They long for ready access to food. He wants to give them access to life. "Do not work for food that spoils," he says, "but for food that endures to eternal life, which the Son of Man will give you" (John 6:27a).

The purpose of our Lenten journey is to draw us to a laser-like focus on Jesus. All our efforts in self-denial and fasting, all our services of compassion to those in need, are for the express purpose of drawing our attention to Jesus. As Jesus said to the gathered crowd, "My Father's will is that everyone who looks to the Son and believes in him shall have eternal life, and I will raise them up at the last day" (v. 40).

Lay aside your vague generalities and focus on Jesus! On this Lord's day, in your worship, lift up your heart and your hands to Christ! He is enough!

—JCM

REFLECTION & PRACTICE

01 The crowd claims to want to understand and perform the works of God. Yet, before they are willing to obey, they demand another sign.

- Are we ever guilty of insisting God prove God's self before we are willing to risk trusting obedience?

02 The crowd references the provision of manna in the desert, wrongly attributing it to Moses instead of God. Their intent seems to be to compare Jesus and his actions to how they as a people have experienced God in the past.

- What parallels can be drawn between the provision of manna and Jesus's miracle of the loaves and fish?
- What is Jesus revealing about his identity when he describes himself as bread from heaven?
- So focused are they on the past actions of God and the bread of yesterday's miracle that the crowd misses Jesus's self-revelation in the moment. What things serve as distractions for us that prevent us from witnessing God's current revelation?

03 Jesus resists the crowd's attempts to make him king by force. Jesus will not be manipulated or distracted from his mission of obedience to the Father. Every generation is guilty of manipulating Jesus by trying to force him into a culturally palatable mold: Jesus as a political dissident, Jesus as a social justice warrior, Jesus as a moral guide, Jesus as a (fill in the blank).

- How do we attempt to shape Jesus into our own mold, formed by our preferences, cultural expectations, and personal causes?
- What would it take to surrender our images of Jesus and submit to the Spirit's revelation of Jesus?
- How might this discipline be more effective when done in community with a diverse, robust collective of Jesus followers?

PRAYER

Lord, we desire to know you and join you in your work in the world. We acknowledge, however, that our desires, well intentioned though they may be, are not always pure. They are colored by our own motives, our own agendas, our own interpretations of who you are or who we think you should be. Unveil the idolatries in our hearts, that we might know you more truly. Humble us, that we might be able to learn from others who know and experience you differently than we do. Above all, empower us to practice trusting obedience even when we do not understand perfectly.

MONDAY

AM *Psalm: 89:1–18*

PM *Psalm: 89:19–52*

Genesis 49:1–28

Mark 7:24–37

1 Corinthians 10:14–11:1

The Gospel text for today finds Jesus moving into territory that was considered hostile. The tensions between Galileans and Phoenicians was high. Yet, when he arrives in Tyre near the Mediterranean coast, he finds that his reputation for healing has gone before him. Though he wants to keep his presence in the area secret, the people spread the word. A Greek woman, born in Syrian Phoenicia, comes to him, falling at his feet. In one of the most awkward exchanges we have in the stories of Jesus, she pleads with him to deliver her daughter from a demon, and he responds with a seemingly harsh refusal: "'First let the children eat all they want,' he told her, 'for it is not right to take the children's bread and toss it to the dogs'" (Mark 7:27).

While we are puzzled by this response, it must not escape us that Jesus is on her turf. Tyre is near the border of Phoenicia. It is not the first time people from that area have seen Jesus's ministry up close. Mark

3:8 indicates that among those in the great crowds that follow Jesus are folk from Tyre and Sidon. In Mark's account of the mission of Jesus, the nearer Jesus comes to the conclusion of his ministry, the more he demonstrates the breadth of his mission. While he came as the Jewish Messiah, his mission is not limited to the narrow confines of Judaism. In this chapter of Mark, he has stepped into the gentile world for an extended time. In this episode in Tyre, and in the healing in the Decapolis of the man who was deaf and dumb, Jesus is outside of Judaism.

The response of Jesus to the Greek woman may be more profound than we can imagine. Her plea to him is in utter desperation for the sake of her daughter. She comes to him with some awareness of what he has been able to do for others. Jesus's disciples and others who follow him may well be in Tyre with him. When the Greek woman approaches, you can almost hear some of them respond with their criticisms: "Who does she think she is? Doesn't she know that gentile women have no right to plead for help from Jewish rabbis?"

Perhaps it is in response to their criticisms that Jesus makes his initial statement to the woman. In her discerning reply, does he see a faith at such a depth that he is determined to acknowledge it? "For such a reply, you may go; the demon has left your daughter" (7:29). Is she free to go back to her gentile world, knowing that things will never be the same? Or is Jesus struggling with the breadth of his mission, still seeking some way to understand what it means for him to be altogether Jewish, yet Savior of the world?

The barrier-breaking Jesus is almost always uncomfortable for us. We prefer predictability and boundaries. Jesus acts with grace and compassion, dismantling our expectations and disregarding boundaries. Perhaps this Lenten season we can open our hearts to see where Jesus may be working outside our boundaries, and join him there!

—JCM

REFLECTION & PRACTICE

01 This is an uncomfortable passage on many levels. We cannot know Jesus's intent behind his usage of the harsh language of the day, "dogs." Is he testing the woman? Is he testing the disciples following his bold condemnation of the abuse of the law of Moses earlier in

the chapter? Or, perhaps, is Jesus himself challenged by the woman's persistence and faith?

- How do we engage challenging texts in healthy ways, avoiding the bitterness of cynicism and the shallowness of uncritical faith?

02 As unsettling as Jesus's initial response to the woman is, what matters is the conclusion. Jesus does not offer the woman the mere crumbs for which she begs. Rather, he offers her abundance: total healing for her child.

- When have you experienced God's unmerited abundance?
- How can we embody this divine extravagance?

03 While the disciples' response is not recorded, we can assume they are shocked by Jesus's engagement with this outsider. She would be considered unclean in every way. In the same way Jesus rejects the abuse of the food laws of Moses by the Pharisees, he also rejects the exclusion of non-Jewish people by extending salvation to a gentile.

- It is uncomfortable to imagine oneself with the exclusive attitude of the disciples or the idolatrous posture toward the law of the Pharisees. Invite the Spirit to search your heart for these attitudes. What individuals or groups evoke anger or disgust in you? Are you in need of confession and repentance?
- How might you intentionally engage in meaningful relationships with those the church might consider outsiders? Have no fear. A feast awaits.

PRAYER

Lord, we do not feign perfect understanding of your work in the world, but we trust your heart. We rest in the assurance that your intent for all of creation is redemption and healing. You do not withhold your goodness. You prepare a feast for us. Grant that we have the persistence of this mother in your presence. May we surrender our prejudice and hard hearts to the transforming work of your Spirit.

TUESDAY

AM *Psalms: 97, 99, 100*

PM *Psalms: 94, 95*

Genesis 49:29–50:14

Mark 8:1–10

1 Corinthians 11:17–34

In the Gospel of Mark, chapters 7 and 8 are pivotal to understanding the objective of the Gospel writer. Over and over again we are confronted with the persistent question, "Do you know who this man Jesus really is?"

The first and most obvious answer is, "This is the Messiah, the Jewish hope, the Son of God."

That begins to dawn on the reader who is carefully following the "plot." The lame are healed. The blind are given sight. The poor and destitute are fed. Demons flee. The gospel of the kingdom is being preached. Jesus is fulfilling many of the hopes and dreams that have grown up around the expectation that God will eventually keep his promise to Israel. The Messianic hope is being stirred again!

But in chapters 7 and 8 the writer begins to make an audacious claim that is difficult to comprehend. After uprooting their understanding of what is clean and how defilement occurs, Jesus leaves the confines of Judaism and moves into hostile gentile territory. The fact that Jesus's reputation is drawing large crowds even in this despised gentile area must be disorienting to the Jewish followers of Jesus. His disciples are still confused by what they are seeing and hearing, and this is only further complicated by the willingness of Jesus to deliver a Greek woman's daughter from demons. He does not then insist that she embrace his Jewishness. He sends her back into her gentile world.

The next phase of his journey takes him again into gentile territory. In the region of the Decapolis, the predominant influence was gentile—pagan, in the minds of the Jews. But it is in this place where Jesus heals a man, probably a gentile, who was deaf and dumb. And then, to the consternation of his disciples, in that same gentile world he feeds four thousand hungry people with the disciples' meager resource of seven loaves and a few fish. Alarm bells should be going off in the minds of the disciples! But they are obtuse enough to miss the whole point.

For the Gospel writer we are in gentile territory, and Jesus is still feeding "his" people. The mission of Jesus is not, was never intended, and should not be today, a mission to the insiders. The question for Jesus was not, "Who is in and who is out?" The kingdom of God question is always, "Who has a need, and what can we do to meet it?"

The image of self-sacrificing love is still hard for us to grasp. In a world consumed with its own needs and wants, the scandal of concern for the welfare—both physical and spiritual—of the outsider is uncomfortably intrusive. It can become so disruptive that even followers of Jesus are divided. Maybe the journey through Lenten repentance is more necessary than we knew.

—JCM

REFLECTION & PRACTICE

01 The disciples' response to Jesus's desire to feed the crowd of gentiles feels absurd. Did they not witness the miraculous provision of God a mere two chapters earlier? Their seeming forgetfulness is almost laughable. Perhaps what looks like doubt of Jesus's ability to provide is actually a resistance against Jesus's compassion to the crowd of outsiders.

- In what ways do we resist the radical inclusion of God?

- How might our resistance hinder our ability to practice compassion for those in need?

02 In the miracle of the bread and loaves performed for the Jewish crowd, twelve baskets of excess were collected, the number twelve calling to mind the twelve tribes of Israel. When the same miracle is performed for the gentile crowd, seven baskets of excess are collected, seven being the number associated with completeness.

- What message might the Gospel writer hope to communicate with this seemingly insignificant detail?
- How might our vision of the church change if we shared the passion of God for *all* to experience the goodness of God, not just those we might deem worthy?

03 Like the crowd in chapter 6 who ate until full, and the gentile mother who begged for crumbs and was given a "feast" of healing, this crowd too is filled to overflowing. God intends abundance for creation. God's saving action is not on a budget.

- How might we be shaped by the myth of scarcity? How does that inform how we interact with others, particularly those who might be considered outsiders?
- Where do you see a need for others to experience the extravagant provision of God, spiritually or materially? How might you be an agent of that provision?

PRAYER

Lord, we give you thanks for setting a place for us at your banquet of salvation. We are overcome by your generosity to us. We confess that our gratitude has not always moved us to act generously toward others. Forgive us for the ways in which we have been agents of exclusion instead of inclusion. Forgive us for choosing self-preservation over self-sacrificial love. Soften our hearts, that we might share in your divine compassion and join you in your work of redemption.

WEDNESDAY

AM *Psalms: 101, 109*

PM *Psalm: 119:121–144*

Genesis 50:15–26

Mark 8:11–26

1 Corinthians 12:1–11

When we are absorbed in distress, confusion, and uncertainty, we can easily miss the helpfully obvious.

When I was a young pilot learning to fly in the mountains of New Mexico, my feisty, experienced, and no-nonsense instructor was relentless in teaching me to concentrate on the essentials. "The three priorities are," she said, "aviate, navigate, and communicate. *In* that order. In *that* order. In that *order*!" It was a mantra I heard almost every day in one way or another. In lay terms: keep the plane in the air, don't run into a mountain, and don't be afraid to ask for help. As a pilot it was my primary responsibility, should a crisis occur, to fly the plane. "Don't be distracted by the problem," she said. "Keep the plane in the air."

Jesus and his disciples are in a boat again, headed back into more familiar, Galilean territory. As they make their way, he is reflecting on his last encounter with Pharisees and their demand for some kind of sign to prove to them that he is the Messiah. Jesus says to the disciples in Mark 8:15, "Be careful. Watch out for the yeast of the Pharisees and that of Herod." The pervasive characteristic of baker's yeast is that it invades and influences every part of the dough in which it is enfolded. Just a little goes a long way. Jesus is saying to the disciples, "If you are not careful, you will be influenced, directed, enticed by the subtle demands and priorities of misguided religion and self-protective empire, and you might miss what is going on before your very eyes."

The disciples have already experienced some remarkable moments with Jesus in a boat on the Sea of Galilee. Now, in a boat again, they are confronted by Jesus as directly as at any other time in their journey together. According to Mark, they have witnessed a remarkable series of divine encounters. The Greek woman's daughter was delivered from demons. A deaf and mute man was healed and released to tell the story. Four thousand people were fed in a remote area in gentile territory with seven loaves of bread and a few small fish. This was the second such miraculous feeding, and the disciples were participants in both.

Now, in the boat, Jesus cautions them to be wary of the yeast of the Pharisees and of Herod—but they are worried that he is criticizing them because they forgot to bring bread onto the boat.

"You are worried about bread?" he asks. "Can't you see? Are you blind to what has been going on right in front of you? Do you remember the bread and the fish?"

We too can become distracted by problems, overwhelming situations, unanswered questions. We can be enticed by voices and cultures that seek to draw our attention away from what is true and good. Yet, in a remarkable twist of grace, Mark tells another healing story. Friends bring a blind man to Jesus, pleading for his healing. In no other account does Jesus's touch not complete a healing. In this case, however, he must touch the man a second time. Mark seems to be insinuating that the disciples—like us—are often blind to what is right before them. Though disappointed and sometimes even frustrated, Jesus continues to reveal himself to the disciples, never giving up, always leading them further toward his mission, his identity, his kingdom. Yes, we are probably missing something too. Just don't miss the grace!

—JCM

REFLECTION & PRACTICE

01 Jesus warns the disciples of the yeast of the Pharisees—the invasive, corrupting power of "misguided religion and self-protective empire."

- Where have you seen the effects of misguided religion? How have we ourselves participated in it? What are the consequences—both inside and beyond the church—of our failure to address the yeast of misguided religion?

- The corrupting nature of power is insidious, leading the undiscerning power holder to retreat into self-protection. The goal becomes maintaining power over stewarding power wisely. As much as the Pharisees look with disdain on the power abuses of Rome, they too hold a white-knuckle grip on power within the community of faith. What is the danger of persisting in an unreflective posture toward the power held by the church? In what ways might we be complicit in clinging to power?

02 The healing of the blind man takes place in two stages. The point is not that Jesus's powers of healing are rusty or that this particular case of blindness is more serious than any other that Jesus has faced. Following the account of the disciples' inability to recognize Jesus and understand his mission, the two-part healing alludes to the persistent nature of blindness.

- What factors contribute to the persistence of our own blindness?

- What values and practices in secular culture and perhaps even in the church reinforce or protect blindness?

03 Neither the blind man nor the disciples can heal their own vision. The blind man requires the touch of Christ, and the disciples the enlightenment of the Spirit.

- How might we make ourselves available to the particular healing we need?

PRAYER

Lord, we acknowledge that we are inattentive to the yeast of subtle demands and priorities of misguided religion and self-preserving empire. We are complicit—sometimes through passive indifference and sometimes through explicit participation—in perpetuating sinful systems and patterns. We are often so blind that we are unaware of the level of our blindness. We long to see rightly, even if the cure is painful, disorienting, or slow in coming. May we be a people who make ourselves open to your healing hand.

THURSDAY

AM *Psalm: 69*

PM *Psalm: 73*

Exodus 1:6–22

Mark 8:27–9:1

1 Corinthians 12:12–26

In the eighth chapter of the Gospel of Mark, Jesus is nearing the completion of his ministry to and with the disciples. He has revealed himself to them in many astounding ways. They are now in the region of Caesarea Philippi, the center of the cult of the emperor as a divine figure. Philip, the son of Herod the Great, inherited this part of his father's kingdom and made Caesarea Philippi his capitol. There was an imposing temple dedicated to worship of the Roman emperor and an impressive headquarters built by Philip. Caesarea Philippi is at the far northern fringe of Jewish territory, twenty-five miles north of the Sea of Galilee. It is fascinating that, according to Mark, this is where Jesus brings his self-revelation to a climax with the disciples.

"Who do people say I am?" he asks them in Mark 8:27. They have been among the people for nearly three years, following Jesus, representing Jesus, and proclaiming the coming of the kingdom of God. They have heard as the people have struggled to know who this remarkable man is who can heal the sick, give sight to the blind, feed thousands from just a few loaves and fish, deliver people from demons, and even raise the dead. Some think that perhaps John the Baptist has come back to life. Others can see shades of the prophet Elijah, the one many assumed would come back to Israel to prepare the way for the appearance of God's Messiah. For others, he is, at the very least, one of the prophets of God.

But Simon Peter—that brash, impulsive fisherman—is the one who gets it: "You are the Messiah!" he cries (8:29). Mark seems to say, "What took you so long?"

Then Jesus begins to prepare them for what lies ahead for him as Messiah: rejection, suffering, death. Then he will be raised! He speaks clearly, forthrightly, and Peter will have nothing of it! Taking Jesus aside he begins to explain to him that Messiahs don't die! Kings conquer! What is he thinking? The words of Peter had a familiar ring to Jesus. He has heard this before. In a moment of stunning response to Peter's words, Jesus cries out, "Get behind me, Satan!" (v. 33).

In our Lenten journey we search for clarity in understanding the suffering death of Jesus. Here we wrestle with the reality that the re-demption of the world is not provided by kneeling before shrines to em-pirical power. The way of redemption is the way of suffering love, where the Son of God has given his life for the redemption of the world. We do not bow before emperors or kings. We kneel at the feet of the Suffering Servant, who—by his death and resurrection—has provided the pathway by which we may walk. We too take up our cross, identify ourselves with his kingdom, and lay down our lives for the needs of others. In so doing, we anticipate the glory of his resurrection as well as our own.

—JCM

REFLECTION & PRACTICE

01 Consider the location of the conversation in this chapter: Caesarea Philippi. Herod the Great sought to curry favor from the Roman emperor by building one of what would become several temples to Caesar in that city. His sons followed suit, seeking to strengthen their own political positions.

- How might this location stir the imaginations of the disciples as they discuss the Messiah?

- How do contemporary expressions of power—whether political, military, or otherwise—subtly influence our understanding of the function and purpose of power?

02 In Jesus's rebuke to Peter, we hear clear echoes of the encounter between Jesus and Satan from three years prior, when Satan tempted Jesus in the wilderness. It is a temptation Jesus has already faced and resisted. In Peter's ignorant attempts to pull Jesus away from the path of suffering to come, he acts as an agent of the powers of darkness.

- When we allow our imaginations to be shaped by secular understandings of power and salvation, we might find ourselves working against the very purposes of God. How do we strengthen our ability to discern between the way of the kingdom and the way of the kingdoms of this world?

03 As the passage continues, Jesus highlights the stark contrast between the way of the empire and the way of the kingdom of God. We have been inoculated against the shock of Jesus's command to carry one's cross, but it would have been alarming and upsetting to the disciples. For them, the command was not merely metaphorical.

- Few, if any, of us will literally carry a cross in obedience to Christ. How might we hide behind the metaphor and resist the call to radical obedience?
- In our success-driven, image-oriented society, to save one's life might be understood as devoting oneself to position, possessions, or power. What might it look like to lose this idolatrous way of life and practice the self-giving, self-sacrificial way of Jesus?

PRAYER

Lord Jesus, we profess that you are the Messiah, the Son of God, sent to redeem creation. Yet we admit that we do not always understand the implications of our own confession. We criticize the disciples' blindness to the upside-down way of the kingdom of God while at the same time calling for the demise of political foes who might threaten our power. Forgive us. Woo us once again back onto the path of faithfulness, that we might embody your self-giving, suffering love.

FRIDAY

AM *Psalm: 107:1–32*

PM *Psalm: 107:33–43*

Exodus 2:1–22

Mark 9:2–13

1 Corinthians 12:27–13:3

If we were watching a movie based on the Gospel of Mark, at this point in the story we would hear the growing volume of drums and music as a climactic movement begins. For eight chapters Mark has been making a point. The reader is listening, following, seeing the unfolding awareness that Jesus is so much more than people realize. Even the disciples, in spite of their constant engagement with Jesus for three years, are not altogether aware of what should be dawning on them. Simon Peter, in a moment of insight, blurted out, "You are the Messiah!" But even still, he was determined that Jesus get it right. He insisted that Jesus understand that Messiahs don't suffer and die.

A few days later Jesus leads Peter, James, and John up on a high mountain. In a moment of stunning revelation, Jesus's clothes begin to glow with an indescribable brilliance, and Elijah and Moses are standing there with him. Then a cloud envelops them, and a voice comes from the cloud: "This is my Son, whom I love. Listen to him!" (Mark 9:7).

It is of no use for us to try to comprehend that moment. We have no corresponding experience or memory that may be used as a means of identification with what happened on that mountain. This is a passage, an account, before which we must simply wait silently, reverently, patiently. God, the I AM, has just spoken. The identity of Jesus as Son of God has been profoundly revealed. His understanding of what it means to be the Messiah is the only one that matters. And the mission he has come to accomplish is moving toward fulfillment.

Our Lenten journey is intended to grip us with a deepening awareness that this is not just another season of the year. We are moving toward the ultimate climax for the redemption of all creation. Our participation in prayer, fasting, repentance and confession, and humble service to others must now begin to bend toward adoration and worship. On this day, in this passage, the incongruity of it all begins to grip us. This is not just a good man dying for other people. This humble, gracious, loving servant, the healer, the restorer of sight and speech, the one before whom storms and waves bow in humility, is much more than Elijah and Moses. This is the Son of God! Yet he will face betrayal, brutality, torture, and the horrendous suffering of death on a cross. Easter morning will only have meaning for us if we get a glimpse of what Peter, James, and John saw that day. It terrified them. Perhaps we ought to be on our faces before him.

—JCM

REFLECTION & PRACTICE

01 On the surface, the transfiguration seems to contradict Jesus's insistent and repetitive predictions of his own suffering and death in preceding chapters. How could one who shares in the very glory of God experience what Jesus has foretold?

- What does this moment of glory unveiled reveal to us about the character of God? Is Jesus's sacrificial act contradictory to his divine nature or an expression of it?

- Theologian and biblical scholar Michael Gorman suggests in *Inhabiting the Cruciform God* that the Philippians 2 passage should be read as "*because* Jesus was in the form of God, he made himself nothing" instead of "although." What's the difference? What does the latter interpretation reveal about God?

02 According to some Jewish tradition and Scripture (see Zechariah 14:16–21), the coming of the Lord would take place during the Festival of Booths, the feast celebrating and remembering Israel's wandering in the wilderness and the Lord's provision. Peter's seemingly random suggestion that they construct booths to live in likely reflects his belief that the year of the Lord has arrived. The ushering in of God's kingdom is now! Peter does not understand that God's kingdom will break in only on the other side of suffering, death, and ultimately resurrection.

- In what ways might we seek to avoid the suffering way of Jesus in our pursuit of the kingdom of God?
- Peter mistakes the sign of transfiguration for the destination. How can we seek out and embody signs of the coming kingdom while always looking forward to full consummation?

03 In the midst of what is a shocking and disorienting experience, one thing is clear: God's command to listen to Jesus. During this Lenten season, how can you be more intentional about listening and obeying?

PRAYER

Lord, we long for the consummation of all things. We ache for your kingdom to come in its fullness. We confess that we often imagine the path to victory as a simple ascent to the mountaintop. We forget that redemption was found not in the glory of the peak but in the bloodstained dust of the valley, in the cold, unforgiving walls of a tomb. May we follow you—to peaks and through valleys—for the sake of your coming kingdom.

SATURDAY

AM *Psalms: 102, 108*

PM *Psalm: 33*

Exodus 2:23–3:15

Mark 9:14–29

1 Corinthians 13:1–13

I have heard 1 Corinthians 13 read at weddings. I have heard it read at Valentine's banquets. I have heard it read at marriage enrichment retreats. I have heard it read at funerals. Could it be, however, that the most significant time to read this chapter is during the journey toward the cross? In a period of deep personal introspection, in this time of spiritual self-examination, these familiar words provide a lens through which we can evaluate our personal investment in what really following Jesus looks like. If following Christ has to do only with our personal salvation—having our ticket punched for heaven—we will probably miss the most significant aspect of the Lenten season. Lent has to do with relationships. One of the duties of our Lenten journey is to evaluate how closely we identify ourselves in likeness to Jesus. One pastor encourages his people to look at Christ, to look at themselves, and to confess the difference.

The words of Paul in the thirteenth chapter of 1 Corinthians create a sense of warmth and appreciation when I think of my relationship with my wife of more than fifty years. We have weathered many a storm, have endured health crises, have wept over family members who strayed or struggled, and have learned how to love each other through the struggle to be authentic, open, forgiving, and affirming. But when I am in the rough and tumble of life in the world and in the church, the words of Paul can become an uncomfortable prick in my soul. How do we live these words in the presence of "the other," whoever that may be? What does it mean in dealing with that person who is so opposite me in personality? And what does it mean in dealing with my enemy, that person who is intent on doing damage and harm to me or my family?

Paul's words are not intended only for the warm and comfortable relationships in our lives. These are instructions to a church deeply divided, constantly at odds, and deeply resistant to the apostle's leadership. They are afflicted by internal strife, immorality at surprising levels, and political division. These Christians—this particular expression of the body of Christ—are a living illustration of the truth that, normally, it is what feeds our pride that divides us.

Tomorrow is the Lord's day. For most who are following this journey, we will be gathering in worship with our local community of faith. Is this a time for confession? Acknowledging where we have failed to love as Paul admonishes us in these words is a step toward healing. But acknowledging it alone is never enough. Amendment of life—or what we call repentance—is the most necessary step. Who knew that such beautiful words could dig so deeply into our souls? But that is Lent for you!

—JCM

REFLECTION & PRACTICE

01 In the economy of society, the most productive, gifted, and successful individuals are highly valued for what they contribute to the greater whole. This economy of usefulness often infects the church. Paul makes clear that any skill, knowledge, or even spiritual practices that are not born from love are worse than useless; they are a detriment.

- Where do we tolerate unloving behavior in our faith communities because we fear losing what that person has or does?

Perhaps they are a generous tither but controlling and manipulative. Perhaps they are a gifted musician but prideful.

- What would it look like to reorient the culture of our churches away from valuing and catering to the usefulness of individuals to valuing and affirming behavior that embodies divine love?

02 Love is often understood in terms of personal benefit. We persist in love as long as we personally gain from the relationship.

- How does the definition of love in this text confront and dismantle any definition of love oriented around self?
- Sit with verses 4–7 for a moment. In which areas might the Spirit be prompting you to confess and repent?

03 Unfortunately, abusers have manipulated this text to prevent the abused separating themselves from toxic relationships by insisting that love endures all things. How might this text, rightly understood, serve as a tool of empowerment and freedom for the abused rather than chains of bondage?

04 Love is a lesson that lasts a lifetime. We will not perfectly embody it this side of eternity. Only when the kingdom comes in its fullness will we see rightly and know fully, as we are already known by God. How can our practice of love, both corporate and individual, be a sign of the in-breaking kingdom of God?

PRAYER

Lord, thank you for your radical love, demonstrated in your life, death, and resurrection. You see us and know us and love us fully. We confess that we have not always modeled well the love we have received. Our pride has led us away from selfless, self-sacrificing love and toward self-promotion and posturing. Forgive us our pride and selfishness, both so often rooted in fear. Cast out the fear of our hearts with your perfect love and empower us to love as we have been loved. May our love be a sign of your kingdom to the world you adore.

FIFTH SUNDAY IN LENT

AM *Psalm: 118*

PM *Psalm: 145*

Exodus 3:16–4:12

Romans 12:1–12

John 8:46–59

My senior year of high school, I had the privilege of participating in an overseas mission trip in Senegal, the country on the westernmost tip of Africa. Our stay overlapped with the celebration of the Tabaski Festival, known as Eid al-Adha in most other Muslim nations. The festival commemorates the obedience of Ibrahim in offering his son Ishmael to God as a sacrifice. (In contrast, Christians affirm the biblical recounting of the story in which Abraham offers his son Isaac to the Lord, not Ishmael.) In honor of Ibrahim's act of trusting obedience, Senegalese families gather together and slaughter a sheep for a family feast.

In the days leading up to the celebration of Tabaski, I noticed the increasing din of the sheep. The sound of bleating and stamping hooves grew as every family in the city bought a sheep and tied it up outside their house or in their courtyard. When the day arrived, the neighborhood sounded like a petting zoo—until the moment arrived. The sacrifices were made. Silence fell.

In Romans 12, Paul encourages his readers to offer their bodies as "living sacrifices" as an act of worship to God. It seems a contradiction in terms. Like the sheep in Senegal, we tend to think of sacrifice as one loud, permanent yes. But Paul is suggesting a different kind of sacrifice: a thousand daily yeses in obedience to God. The problem with living sacrifices, as my college chaplain once told me, is that they tend to crawl off the altar. The call of Christian discipleship is to fix oneself to the altar in daily submission. Dramatic, singular acts of obedience are of value, but a life of faithfulness is better measured by the small, consistent yeses to Jesus in the ordinary days that make up our lives.

Paul goes on to describe the life of a living sacrifice. What is the hallmark of a life lived in continual submission to God? Right relationship with others, first and foremost in the community of faith. To follow Jesus, we cannot be consumed in ourselves but ought to understand ourselves in the context of the Christian community. We can only understand ourselves rightly in the context of the church. We reject the philosophy of this world that tries to convince us of our autonomy, independence, and lack of responsibility for one another. Our identity and vocation are inextricably intertwined with that of our sisters and brothers of faith. Paul continues describing what the life of a living sacrifice looks like: genuine love, a vehement rejection of evil, a white-knuckled grip on goodness. Lift one another up, highlighting the successes and gifts of others. Persevere in faithfulness, regardless of the cost.

During the Lenten season, we focus our hearts and minds on the faithfulness of God in Christ. As those who have been invited to be conformed to the image of that faithful Son, let us embrace this call to offer our lives as living sacrifices and, as faith communities, embody sacrificial love for the sake of the world.

—*SDL*

REFLECTION & PRACTICE

01 Romans 12 is a much-quoted passage of Scripture. At first glance, it seems straightforward and uncomplicated. But at a deeper level, it

can become troubling, especially in light of the fact that living sacrifices can "crawl off the altar."

- How can we read this chapter from a different perspective? Where might the emphasis be shifted to make us more aware of the challenge that Paul is issuing the church in Rome?
- Read Romans 11:33–36. How does that passage provide greater meaning to the admonition in Romans 12?

02 Paul challenges readers to offer our bodies as a living sacrifice and then immediately cautions us to humility.

- Why do you think he turns so quickly to that admonition?
- How is this humility exercised within the body of Christ?

03 In most Bible translations there is a paragraph break at verse 9. It may appear to some that the admonition to love has to do with what follows.

- Does the admonition to love sincerely speak only to what follows? How might it speak to the preceding verses as well?
- How does the invitation to love sincerely relate to the first two verses of this chapter?
- How does Jesus demonstrate what it means to be a living sacrifice, to walk humbly, and to love sincerely? How does that inform our living?

PRAYER

Lord, our deepest hunger during this journey is to know you better, to identify ourselves with your self-giving love. Thank you for the admonitions of your servant Paul. May we not leave those words as poetic sentiments on a page, but may our lives reflect our increasing hunger to know you better and to become more like you in every way.

MONDAY

AM *Psalm: 31*

PM *Psalm: 35*

Exodus 4:10–31

Mark 9:30–41

1 Corinthians 14:1–19

A recurring theme in the Gospel of Mark is unexpected reversal. What the disciples expect to hear, even what they assume to be true, is often turned on its head. The poor deserve to be that way. Blindness is evidence of sin. The leper is to be shunned and avoided. Good people don't associate with sinners. Women and all other outsiders should stay outside. Messiahs should act like Messiahs! There is no room for humility, compassion, patience, or love. Call out the warriors with swords and spears. Above everything else, when you are going to take on the empire, be the strongest, the best armed, and the meanest. Otherwise, you could end up on a cross, and that would be the end of everything!

It is not really surprising that the disciples of Jesus are confused and disoriented. The longer they spend with Jesus, the more convinced they are that he could be the Messiah. But every expectation they have about what that means is being challenged, overturned, and undermined. He keeps coming back to that confusing idea about being crucified on a cross. It just doesn't make sense! But if he is going to be the Messiah, however he intends to do it, they want to be sure who sits where in the Messiah's cabinet! Who deserves to be first? Who comes from the right family tree? Who is smartest, strongest, most respected? It's the normal thing to do, to be sure you get your due.

And then Jesus does it again. He calls a young child—a worthless being in the eyes of the culture. Children are expendable. They should certainly be seen and not heard. But Jesus takes the child in his arms. I can see it in my mind. His loving embrace is a delicious expression of grace to a child, even while it is a shocking demonstration of misplaced priorities to the disciples. Everything is turned upside down. They have just been arguing about who will be first in the new kingdom Jesus is going to inaugurate, and Jesus is demonstrating the very nature of that kingdom.

We continue on this journey toward Jesus's enthronement. The disciples are desperate that Jesus get this Messiah business done right, and Jesus is intent on showing them that this is not going to be your everyday empire. His is a kingdom of grace, mercy, and compassion. His is to be a kingdom where the last are first and the first last. His is to be a kingdom where the blind see, the hungry are fed, and the diseased are healed. His throne is not to be a gilded chair in a palace but a wooden cross on a hill. He is not going to overthrow Caesar. He is going to crush Satan. He is not intending to overwhelm the power of an army. He is going to destroy the power of sin. Are they beginning to catch on? Are we?

—JCM

REFLECTION & PRACTICE

01 Jesus explicitly explains his impending death for the second time. The disciples do not understand and, according to the text, are "afraid to ask him" (Mark 9:32). As the subsequent verses will reveal, the disciples are focused on their positions in the coming kingdom. Perhaps their pride and desire to appear wise keep them from humbly seeking understanding.

- How does our pride prevent us from seeking understanding?
- How might humbly acknowledging our shortcomings and imperfect knowledge free us from fear?

02 Jesus's simple inquiry about the disciples' discussion concerning who is the greatest is met with silence, revealing their shame. While they do not fully understand Jesus's mission or method, they recognize the incongruity of their discussion with the way of the teacher.

- Think of a time the Spirit highlighted incongruity in you—a pattern or habit that did not align with the way of Jesus. How did you respond to that prompting?
- Shame often incites us to hide instead of seeking the healing and forgiveness we need. How might you pay attention when shame pops up unexpectedly? What might God want to heal or transform in you?

03 In contrast to the disciples' discussion about being the greatest, Jesus draws a vulnerable child to himself. To welcome the vulnerable, the lowly, or those considered of less value for their inability to pull their own weight is to welcome Jesus and the One who sent him.

- Who are the vulnerable and the less valued around you? What would it look like to actively welcome them?
- How might the local body of Christ of which you are a part practice hospitality to the vulnerable in your community?

PRAYER

Lord, we confess the incongruity of our hearts and lives with the way of your kingdom. Often our values, habits, and desires are misshapen by our pride and desire for position and power. But you do not measure value as we do. You open your arms to the weak, the vulnerable, those unable to do for themselves. Help us to recognize both our role in welcoming the vulnerable and powerless but also our place among them. Through our weakness and insufficiency confessed, you are proven strong. Humble us, that you might be glorified.

TUESDAY

AM *Psalms: 121, 122, 123*

PM *Psalms: 124, 125, 126*

Exodus 5:1–6:1

Mark 9:42–50

1 Corinthians 14:20–40

If ever we are going to take sin seriously, this is the season to do so. We gaze into the deepening darkness, stunned all over again at what Jesus endured in his betrayal, trial and torture, and crucifixion. Mel Gibson's movie *The Passion of the Christ* has become, for many, the depiction of the sufferings of Jesus that wrenched their imagination away from a casual disregard for what Jesus might have actually experienced. The scriptural descriptions of what he endured are mercifully sparse. While the movie is graphic and stunningly brutal, much of what is depicted is, at best, cinematic imagination. Our efforts at empathy—at seeking somehow to understand what Jesus endured—are futile. While we can appreciate that he endured such agony on our behalf, it is far too easy to be lulled into a dismissal of the destructive power of sin and the seriousness with which Jesus approached it.

The words of our passage in Mark are not easy for us to embrace. We don't like to think about sin or its consequences in our culture. We prefer religion that is nice, accepting, filled with grace, hope, peace, and love. While that is not wrong, left to that alone it is altogether inadequate. It does not acknowledge the destructive capacity of sin, both individually and collectively. But Jesus will not allow the disciples to disregard the mortal danger of ignoring sin. They are living demonstrations of the human capacity to wallow in self-interest. Though Jesus has done and said all he can to reorient their worldview, to challenge their assumptions, to shake them loose from the unbelief that so blinds them to his identity and the purpose of his coming, they are still arguing about who among them is the greatest.

Sin is blinding. And the greatest blindness is the unwillingness to see what is at stake when we are oblivious to the damage we do to others when we either diminish their value or disregard our responsibility for their well-being. The warning Jesus gives his disciples is pointed, direct, and unflinching. Scholars are divided as to whom Jesus is referring to when he says "one of these little ones" (Mark 9:42). Is it the children he has gathered around him? Is it the disciples or the other followers of Jesus? Whatever the determination, there is danger—grave and eternal danger—in wounding or spiritually misleading others.

As direct as he is, Jesus does not leave the disciples hopeless or without guidance. In this reference, salt has to do with character, with being transformed by their connection with Jesus. He makes it clear: character is forged in the fire. The hard places can either distract us or form us. The flavoring, preserving nature of salt is an image of what they are intended to become.

This Lenten journey may well take us through the fire. Lean into the flames, and let the Christ who suffered for us purge us, flavor us, and deploy us.

—JCM

REFLECTION & PRACTICE

01 Putting a stumbling block in front of the little ones described by Mark has often been understood as leading someone into sinful behavior. But what if stumbling blocks are not always so explicit? What if the most harmful thing we could do to someone's faith is

to proclaim the way of Jesus while not embodying the way of Jesus? Even as they follow Jesus, the disciples persist in self-promotion, protecting their position and power.

- What stumbling blocks do our lives inadvertently create for others seeking Jesus? Do we live selfishly? Are we known for political partisanship more than for our love of and obedience to Jesus? Do we have a reputation as unforgiving or judgmental?
- Has someone ever put a stumbling block on your path of faith with their disobedience? How did that experience impact your faith?
- Consider the individuals who have modeled humble obedience for you. Whom might you influence in this way?

02 Jesus is certainly not calling his followers to self-mutilation. Rather, he is calling us to examine the things in our lives that habitually lead us into sin. With surgical precision, those things must be removed. This is not a matter of legalism but of the heart. What do we love more? The habits, patterns, and relationships that continually lead us astray, or faithfulness to Jesus and his way?

- Be honest with yourself. What habits, practices, relationships, etc., misshape your heart and devotion? What would it look like to remove the hand or the eye?

03 Salt is versatile. It has been used to clean wounds and functions as an agent of healing. It also preserves food, protecting it form spoiling. We both need the work of salt within us and are mysteriously also called to be salt.

- Where might you need the healing work of salt in your life? What wounds are you carrying that need the attention of the Spirit?
- The work of salt is effective but often painful and difficult to endure. As you respond to the Spirit's invitation to healing and wholeness, who might support you through the process with love and encouragement?
- Jesus expands the metaphor and calls his disciples to be salt. How might you be an agent of healing in the lives of others?

Where might those around you need the preserving, protecting work of your faithful obedience and witness?

PRAYER

Lord, thank you for speaking difficult words to us. In your great love, you do not leave us as we are. You call out our unfaithfulness, our hypocrisy, our self-deception. You invite us to throw away those things that lead us astray, not to enforce a new legalism but to set our hearts free to love and follow you more faithfully. We confess our deep and continual need for your healing and cleansing work in our lives. As radical as it seems to us, we recognize that even as you heal us, you call us to be agents of healing. Even as you forgive and cleanse us, you invite us to be agents of reconciliation. May we heed your call to obedience and join you in the work of redemption with joy and gratitude.

WEDNESDAY

AM *Psalm: 119:145–176*

PM *Psalms: 128, 129, 130*

Exodus 7:8–24

Mark 10:1–16

2 Corinthians 2:14–3:6

Jesus was the ultimate expression of the covenant-keeping God. His incarnation was evidence that God intended to redeem creation and establish a relationship of deepest intimacy between himself and humankind. In the life and ministry of Jesus we see the passion of God for keeping the covenant he made with Abraham in Genesis 15, whatever the cost.

During the era in which Jesus lived as Israel's Messiah, divorce was as widespread as it is today. Roman law gave easy latitude for divorce, heavily favoring men. The Pharisees came to Jesus to test him, said Mark. The painful reality is that, in Judaism, the twisting of the law made divorce as accessible as in the Roman culture at large, with the advantage given to men.

Jesus quickly recasts the entire conversation. The permission given by Moses was actually a concession intended to curb the abuses of a husband merely dismissing a wife. A certificate was necessary as a protection for the vulnerability that occurred when a man found some reason to be displeased with his wife. A divorce certificate to prove she was no longer married made the woman able to move forward with at least a minimal level of protection. But God never provided for divorce, says Jesus. From the beginning marriage was to be a covenant of faithfulness. The man and the woman were to leave father and mother, be joined together as husband and wife, and become one flesh. And each was equally responsible for maintaining and preserving that covenant of faithfulness.

The journey toward the cross Jesus was making with his disciples was a demonstration of the in-breaking kingdom of God. In this kingdom the values of this current world are turned upside down. The pattern for the kingdom was the covenant faithfulness of God and the unceasing love of Jesus. The self-serving, advantage-seeking, power-grabbing way of life that so characterized the world were of no interest to Jesus. The way into his kingdom was not the way of money, sex, or power. In order to enter his kingdom one had to come like a little child—vulnerable, gentle, powerless. It flew in the face of everything the disciples of Jesus had been taught all their lives. Tax collectors, zealots, and fishermen survived by advantage, violence, and hard work. But Jesus said, "Stop. Breathe. Trust."

The disciples were not there yet. But, given our advantage of two thousand years of hindsight and six weeks of study and prayer, perhaps we are getting closer. The brokenness that so characterized the world of those first disciples continues. The destruction and trauma of broken relationships and overwhelming guilt are as real today as they were then. But there is hope. The reason Jesus went to the cross was to break the destructive power of sin and to provide for a new way of being in this world. That is why he came. Lean into that!

Stop. Breathe. Trust.

—JCM

REFLECTION & PRACTICE

01 Even as the religious leaders attempt to catch Jesus violating the covenant between God and God's people, they themselves are violating the spirit of the covenant by perpetuating abuses in human covenant

relationships. Does our practice of the law of God ever come into conflict with the spirit of the law of God?

02 While a broken marriage covenant goes against the intent of God for the marriage relationship, God demonstrates God's passion to protect and provide for the vulnerable and powerless by providing the concession for the regulation of divorce.

- What does this concession reveal about God's heart for the weakest among us?
- If God is willing to act in this way on behalf of the vulnerable, how might we be called to do the same?

03 God's desire that marriage might be a reflection of God's covenant with humankind indicates that our marital relationships should be marked by sacrificial self-giving, vulnerability, and mutuality.

- How do these defining traits of a covenantal relationship stand in contrast to the expectations of intimate relationships in secular culture?
- How might these same traits be put into practice in non-marital relationships?

04 Life lived in light of the in-breaking kingdom of God is not marked by pride, power, or a search for loopholes but by humility, with hands outstretched to receive what we cannot create or conjure on our own.

- How does this intentional embrace of humility and acknowledgment of our need conflict with the self-sufficient, self-preserving narratives around us?
- How might our relationships be transformed if we assumed the posture of the vulnerable, humble child, at peace with our need and with the One who can meet it?

PRAYER

Lord, thank you for your unending faithfulness to your covenant with creation. From the beginning of time, you have set about righting the brokenness wrought by sin and death. You persist in the face of our apathy and unfaithfulness. Though our pride and self-promoting behaviors often hinder us, we desire our relationships with one another to reflect the covenant you have made with us. Forgive us when we rebel and seek our own good at the expense of others. Cleanse us from self-serving patterns and return us to the path of self-giving love.

THURSDAY

AM *Psalms: 131, 132, 133*

PM *Psalms: 140, 142*

Exodus 7:25–8:19

Mark 10:17–31

2 Corinthians 3:7–18

We are shaped by the cultural assumptions that surround us, so it can be disorienting when we are confronted by a truth in our Christian journey that challenges those assumptions. Sometimes it is so disorienting that we feel wronged—even betrayed.

When the rich man comes running up to Jesus in today's passage, the disciples are stunned by Jesus's response to the man. He is a good man. He has kept the law and has been faithful in fulfilling everything that is expected of him as a son of the law. "We need a man like that," the disciples are likely thinking. But Jesus's words to him are like a dagger to his heart. "One thing you lack. Go, sell everything you have and give to the poor" (Mark 10:21b). The incongruity for the disciples occurs because, in their understanding of how things work, wealth is evidence of the blessing of God. This man's life is a living testimony that God blesses the good with wealth! For all his enthusiasm to hear what Jesus has to say, the man goes away sad *because* he has great wealth. Perhaps the words of Jesus would be more easily understood if we read it, "Go, sell everything that has you."

Note that Mark tells us Jesus loves the man. He sees the man's potential, the hunger of his heart, and wants what is best for him. His response to the man is not mean-spirited or harsh, but it is direct and truthful. Jesus is not saying there is anything innately sinful in having possessions. Many of the people of God in the Old Testament were very wealthy. Among the people who accompany Jesus in his ministry are some women who are wealthy enough that they provided for Jesus and the disciples "out of their own means" (Luke 8:3). Instead, the challenge of Jesus has to do with where we place our trust. He has already made clear that coming into the kingdom of God is by way of humility and trust. We can only enter when we come as children, laying aside all our pride in standing, position, and possessions. But when we do enter in this way, nothing of lasting value is forfeited. "Love each other as I have loved you," Jesus says in John 15:12. Everything about his life and ministry embodies those words. He asks nothing of his disciples that he has not demonstrated in his own journey.

As we walk through this Lenten journey, allow the incongruity of it all to sweep over you. Don't ignore it. Face it. Maybe the most important question to ask ourselves is, "What has me?" To what is your heart and/or your mind so attached that to follow the way of Jesus threatens your well-being? Maybe it is time to let it go.

—JCM

REFLECTION & PRACTICE

01 Jesus makes clear that wealth is not a measure of God's favor. While we mentally assent to this teaching, our lives do not always reflect agreement.

- How do we, consciously or unconsciously, perpetuate the belief that material blessing is indicative of God's favor?
- What would it look like to unhitch the cart of God's favor from external indicators of blessing? How might this practice change how we see ourselves and others?

02 Jesus also makes clear that keeping the letter of the law does not necessarily indicate a heart and life given fully over to the Lord. Based on Jesus's response to the rich man, what postures, behaviors, or attitudes might indicate a heart and life given fully over to the Lord?

03 Jesus's command to sell everything is a judgment not on wealth but on a reliance on wealth that overshadows trust in God.

- How does what is good, or morally neutral, often become a stumbling block in our lives?
- What practices can guide us in maintaining our heart's devotion rightly fixed?

PRAYER

Lord, like the rich man, we desire to receive and participate in the coming age of your kingdom. We confess, however, that desire is often thwarted or dulled by other devotions. Our hearts are so easily won by wealth, position, and power. Forgive us and heal our sin-sick hearts, that we might love you more fully and follow you more faithfully, no matter the cost. To be one with you is the supreme good.

FRIDAY

AM *Psalm: 22*

PM *Psalms: 141, 143*

Exodus 9:13–35

Mark 10:32–45

2 Corinthians 4:1–12

We love the idea of celebrity. We like to be around celebrities. We put them on platforms, buy their music, and read their books. We wear their jerseys and draft them on our fantasy teams. We tout them as worthy of our adulation. We make heroes of them. Many parents hope their children might become celebrities. We want to be seen with and connected to celebrities, even if we are not celebrities ourselves.

Jesus was evaluated by some as one of those celebrities we should like to be around. He could work wonders. People were healed, sight was restored. Banquets grew out of lunch bags. Crowds grew. But whenever Jesus spoke to his disciples privately, he warned them that this was not what the future held for him or for them. He often cautioned people to whom he had ministered to keep what he had done for them a secret.

In today's Mark passage, Jesus tells his disciples for the third time what lies ahead for him. It is clear. He knows what is coming. It is also clear that they are still obstinately blind to the true meaning of his words. They are so blind that it does not occur to James and John, two of his three inner-circle disciples, that their self-serving request for honored positions is a denial of everything Jesus has been teaching them for the past three years. In their request, they also leave their friend Peter to fend for himself in seeking any position of significance. "We want to sit at your right hand and your left hand when you come into your glory," they say.

The irony of their request is that Jesus's glory would not be revealed by his being seated on a throne. It would be revealed by his being nailed to a cross, and the people selected to sit on his left and his right would be two thieves. That is Jesus's glory. On the cross he bore all the sin and agony of humanity, suffering on our behalf, redeeming us, purchasing our redemption through his wounds. That is how he revealed that his kingdom was unlike the kingdoms and empires of this world. The world's structures are built on dominance, achievement, possession, power, and hierarchy. In Jesus's kingdom the power is found in suffering love, in mutual submission, in service to one another.

As Jesus says to James and John, in this world the rulers "lord it over" their subjects. "Not so with you," says Jesus (Mark 10:42, 43). This is a different way of being in the world. Here, the way up is down. The way to greatness is suffering love. The way to power is relinquishment. The way to glory is humble service to the broken and the powerless. Such service, said Paul to the Corinthians, is only possible when the life of Jesus is revealed in us (2 Corinthians 4:10). Let's step out of the spotlight in order that we might reflect his light.

—JCM

REFLECTION & PRACTICE

01 Self-promotion is not a practice restricted to celebrities and politicians. All of us do it. We promote ourselves or our accomplishments to gain the attention and approval of others. As Christians, we cloak our self-promotion in language of piety and humility but to the same end: recognition.

- Where have you seen this pattern at play in your own heart and life?
- While many of us cannot remove ourselves completely from the platforms that encourage self-promotion, we can model a

different way of being. How might followers of Jesus practice genuine, Christlike humility?

02 The request of James and John is shocking in its boldness, yet it reflects a universal human desire: to secure one's place. We hunger—not only for position and recognition but also for security. We fear there will not be enough or that we will be forgotten and left behind.

- How has the desire for security and the fear of scarcity influenced your behavior, consciously or unconsciously?
- How do we seek healing from these fears? What is the way out of being controlled by our desire for security and place?

03 Our fearful pursuit of position and security damages our relationship with God and with others. Once again, Jesus invites his disciples to a new way of life that reflects the kingdom of God values of service and self-sacrifice. This way of being in the world transforms our relationships from competitions to cooperation for the sake of one another.

- How has self-promotion and pursuit of position or recognition damaged relationships in your life?
- Where might you need to repent of these fears and desires and go a new way? How might your relationship with others be transformed as you embody the self-giving way of Jesus?

PRAYER

Lord, we confess that we often fall into the pattern of self-promotion and self-preservation. We fear scarcity, or that we will be forgotten. We strive after recognition and approval from others to demonstrate our worth. We stand in need of both forgiveness and healing. You invite us to abandon the hustle and instead pick up a cross in service to others. Purify the desires of our hearts, that we might hunger after that which pleases you.

SATURDAY

AM *Psalms: 137, 144*

PM *Psalms: 12, 13*

Exodus 10:21–11:8

Mark 10:46–52

2 Corinthians 4:13–18

Can Jesus trust you with a question? James and John came to Jesus with a very specific request that put Jesus on notice that there were some things he should be willing to do if we ask him. His response to them was a simple, straightforward question: "What do you want me to do for you?" (Mark 10:36).

Today that same question is asked again, in an adjoining account. This time it is to a blind man, Bartimaeus, or "son of Timaeus." There is no indication as to who Timaeus may be, but the implication is obvious: Bartimaeus is on his own. His survival depends on his ability and willingness to beg. No one else is looking out for him. When he hears that Jesus of Nazareth is walking by, he cries out in desperation, "Jesus, Son of David, have mercy on me!" (v. 47).

For those around Jesus, the blind man is an intrusion. They have places to go, and the crowd is intent on hearing Jesus. But he is attentive to a desperate cry for help, and he says to those who have tried to quiet the man, "Call him" (v. 49). He comes running, and Jesus asks that same simple, straightforward question: "What do you want me to do for you?" (v. 51).

In Matthew's account of the request of James and John, their mother came with them to Jesus. She was looking out for her boys. She wanted the best for them and was unafraid to ask for favor. In this account, the brothers came on their own, but they came together, each standing in support of the other. There is no one who will or can look out for Bartimaeus. The brothers asked for privilege, a place at Jesus's side. Bartimaeus asks for mercy. He wants a touch from Jesus's hand. He desperately wants and needs sight.

The two requests made in response to Jesus's simple question stand in stark contrast. The brothers were rebuffed by Jesus. They had to face the anger of the other disciples for their crass attempt at gaining advantage. But Bartimaeus's request is granted, and he receives his sight, the fulfillment of his desperate need. In gratitude he follows Jesus along the road, no doubt singing and shouting praise.

Mark has made a powerful point. The brothers—disciples of Jesus, part of the Twelve—are blind! They still don't get it. Bartimaeus can see what they cannot, and he follows Jesus on the way, no doubt finding other beggars and blind folk, telling them what happened.

How might we respond to that simple question from Jesus? The brothers wanted favor. Bartimaeus wanted sight. What would we request? Given what we have come to know about Jesus and his kingdom, by now we could well be aware that the best response we could give would be to ask on behalf of others. If we get this right, the kingdom of God opens for us and life is given meaning and direction that are not available anywhere else.

Get ready! He will ask the question!

—JCM

REFLECTION & PRACTICE

01 James, John, and Bartimaeus each have a request of Jesus. Jesus invites the men to express their desires freely, but he only grants the request of Bartimaeus. The problem with the two disciples is not that they make a request of the Lord but that their request reveals selfish hearts. What do our desires reveal about the state of our hearts?

02 The request of the brothers and the request of Bartimaeus highlight the difference between people blinded by privilege and a person struggling on the margin of society. The brothers pursue self-promotion while the blind man seeks only mercy—the privilege of human dignity and inclusion.

- Allow these two contrasting narratives to read you. Do you find yourself in pursuit of position and security, or are you hungry for the mercy of God to heal and restore you?
- If we are in a position of privilege, how might we advocate for those on the margins in our petitions of the Lord?

03 The response of the other disciples to the brothers' request is indignation and jealousy. If we were to present our heart's desire to Jesus, would others be repelled by us and perhaps by faith altogether, or would they be more drawn to Jesus?

04 Imagine Jesus standing before you. He asks, "What do you want me to do for you?" How do you respond?

PRAYER

Lord, you know our hearts better than we know them ourselves. Our desires are so often shaped by selfishness and unholy hunger after what does not satisfy. All the while, many around us suffer from lack of simple needs: food, medical care, human dignity. Forgive us for our limited vision. Heal our vision, that we might see you and others rightly. Heal our hearts, that we might desire rightly and come before you with requests that honor you and bless others.

PALM SUNDAY/ SIXTH SUNDAY IN LENT

AM *Psalms: 24, 29*

PM *Psalm: 103*

Zechariah 9:9–12; 12:9–13:9

Luke 19:41–48

1 Timothy 6:12–16

Palm Sunday is always a challenge for pastors. The choice between an emphasis on the Palm Sunday parade in Jerusalem or on the Passion Sunday passage provides a perpetual dilemma. We love the palm branches being waved, children marching through the sanctuary, everyone singing hymns of praise. But we also know that Palm Sunday is the last Sunday before Easter, and for many, the last opportunity to emphasize the Suffering Servant and the sacrificial love of Jesus.

Today's Lenten passages walk the tightrope. There is the magnificence of Psalm 29, where the glory of God as revealed in nature is celebrated: "And in his temple all cry, Glory!" (v. 9). In Luke 19 we read of the moments following the triumphal entry of Christ into Jerusalem with the crowd shouting his praise. "As he approached Jerusalem and saw the city, he wept over it and said, 'If you, even you, had only known on this day what would bring you peace—but now it is hidden from your eyes" (vv. 41–42).

On this Sunday, as we enter Holy Week, we twenty-first-century Christians must hold the tension between praise and grief. Because we know the story, we can sing with the crowds who followed Jesus, our hearts lifted in worship: "Blessed is the king who comes in the name of the Lord! Peace in heaven and glory in the highest!" (Luke 19:38). In spite of what we know is coming this week, we are still able to lift our hearts because, as Zechariah declared, we are "prisoners of hope" (Zechariah 9:12)! Yet still there is the haunting reality that Jesus will face the agony of the cross, and as Jesus said, Jerusalem itself will eventually be sacked, burned, and utterly destroyed.

In many ways we live this Palm Sunday tension throughout our Christian journey. There are moments of praise, of breathless joy and adoration, of thanksgiving to God for his faithfulness and love. We must watch for these moments. We dare not try to create them or force them. They come in the journey as we worship, as we read the Word, as we join with the community of faith in sharing the sacraments, and as we serve the needs of the least and the last. This joy, this adoration and praise, are byproducts of trust, resting ourselves in Christ, even in the face of painful losses. Sometimes joy and adoration are gifts of grace that come seemingly out of nowhere, like a stunning sunset, the majesty of nature, or the first smile of recognition from our new child. And there are searing moments of pain, like a sudden illness that comes from nowhere, the loss of a loved one, a deep and indescribable betrayal, the wound of a friend who walks away, never to return, or—perhaps most deeply—the stunning weight of conviction when we face our own failure and realize the pain we have brought to others.

This is why this day matters. Worship. Praise. Repent. Grieve. In whatever order necessary. Calvary covers it all.

—JCM

REFLECTION & PRACTICE

01 We live in the tension of the unconsummated kingdom of God. We experience great joy and bear witness to redemption at work among us. But we also face great loss and pain as a result of the brokenness that still exists in creation and in our own hearts.

- How have you experienced the tension between joy and sorrow, celebration and mourning?
- How might the tension of Palm Sunday serve as a guide for our spirits as we navigate these difficult seasons?

02 To blindly cling to moments of triumph while ignoring the hurts of life is dangerous. But it is equally perilous to our spirits to see only the brokenness and pain and neglect the goodness of God breaking in all around us. Both tendencies can lead to idolatry.

- Are you more prone to fixate on the negative and ignore God's redemption among us or to deny the powers of sin and death in creation and naively climb from victory to victory? How might this tendency lead to idolatry?
- As you surrender your tendencies and wounds to the Lord, how might God reveal Godself in new ways?

03 Wherever we find ourselves, whether in a season of joy or one of sorrow, in clarity or confusion, we can be assured that Christ is King. While he might not be the kind of king we expected, he is the King we need. How might you rest more fully in the knowledge of Jesus's eternal reign?

PRAYER

Jesus, in many ways, you are not the king we wanted, but you are the King we need. To you we cry out, "Hosanna! Save us." Unshackle our hearts, that we might love and serve you and one another more faithfully. We do not claim to perfectly understand you, but we will seek to perfectly obey you. Pour out your Spirit upon us, that we may see you and what you're doing in us and around us more clearly. Hosanna, hosanna. Come, King Jesus.

MONDAY OF HOLY WEEK

AM *Psalm: 51*

PM *Psalm: 69:1–23*

Lamentations 1:1–12

Mark 11:12–25

2 Corinthians 1:1–7

The final week of Lent draws us nearer and deeper into the passion of Christ. The scriptures are somber, and sometimes we are made aware again of the awful power of sin. David's plea for forgiveness, expressed so profoundly in Psalm 51, appropriately prepares us to face our own complicity in the sufferings of Christ. As the hymn writer John S. B. Monsell put it in 1863, "My sins, my sins, my Savior! How sad on thee they fall."

Sometimes the sin we must face is not outspoken rebellion and debauchery. It is rather the utter blindness of a refusal to believe. Today's passage in Mark is the account of Jesus entering the temple, overturning tables, and driving out those who are desecrating it. They are occupying the space intended for gentiles who wish to worship, filling it with tables, money changers, animals, and other merchandise. His message is clear: "Is it not written: 'My house will be called a house of prayer for all nations'? But you have made it 'a den of robbers'" (Mark 11:17). This infuriates the chief priests and teachers of the law, and they begin in earnest to look for a way to kill him.

The image of that event is lodged in the memory of most people who are followers of Jesus. And we understand the righteous anger of Jesus, at some level. But it is easy to miss the profound meaning of the enacted parable that bookends the temple episode. The previous day was Jesus's first entry into Jerusalem. We call the remembrance of that day Palm Sunday. In today's account he is again entering the city. He spent the night in Bethany and is making his way back to Jerusalem. Mark says he is hungry. Spotting a fig tree covered with leaves, he goes to find out if it has any fruit on it. Interestingly, Mark says it is not the season for fruit. However, finding no fruit, Jesus curses the fig tree! "May no one ever eat fruit from you again" (11:14). The next morning, as Jesus and his disciples are going along, they spot the fig tree withered from the roots, and Peter says, "Look! The fig tree you cursed has withered!" (v. 21).

What is this all about? It is not about our ability, if we have enough faith, to move trees and mountains by our prayers. It is not about the faith of Jesus. This enacted parable is about the judgment of Jesus on the unbelief of the Jewish leaders and the failure of the temple culture to fulfill its purpose. "You did not recognize the time of God's coming to you," Jesus said in Luke 19:44. We must get this right. Sin destroys. And the most destructive sin is the refusal to see and embrace what God is doing and what God has prepared us to do. Israel was given the responsibility to be a light to the nations. Instead, they had become fruitless figs, of no value to the mission for which they were created. "All the splendor has departed from Daughter Zion," wrote Jeremiah (Lamentations 1:6a). Now the Light has walked into the temple, and those who should be most aware of who he is are blinded by their refusal to receive him. But Jesus makes this promise: those who see will be demonstrations of the new kingdom, trusting deeply and practicing radical forgiveness, turning the world upside down.

Let's get this right.

—JCM

REFLECTION & PRACTICE

01 Jesus is enraged to see the place reserved for gentile prayer being used for other purposes.

- Why is this pattern of behavior particularly offensive in the people of God?
- In what ways do we, the church, prioritize what we think is central to faithful worship while missing the heart of God entirely?

02 The lesson of the fig tree seems strange and disparate from the rest of the text, but in light of the entire story of God, Jesus's meaning becomes clear. Israel is consistently represented by a fig tree. Obedience results in flourishing; rebellion results in withering. Obedience produces nourishing fruit for others; rebellion benefits no one, not even the tree itself.

- We often think of obedience and its results as limited to us or our small circle of influence. How might our obedience, or lack thereof, have a wider impact?
- Imagine a life marked by obedience and submission to God's call. Who might be nourished by the fruit of your obedience?

03 The religious leaders are so blind to what God is doing that they do not realize how truly rotten their fig tree is. Is it possible that we might be blind to what God is doing on occasion? What is the test of our fruit?

PRAYER

Lord, how often do we gather to worship you, oblivious to our own idolatries? How often do we give ourselves over to the practices of religion and miss your very heart for the world? Forgive our blindness, our pride, and our self-righteousness. We want to flourish, not for our own sake but to nourish the world you love. Prune us gently, lest we despair. We submit our branches to your care.

TUESDAY OF
HOLY WEEK

AM *Psalms: 6, 12*

PM *Psalm: 94*

Lamentations 1:17–22

Mark 11:27–33

2 Corinthians 1:8–22

Presumed authority can be a dangerous thing. As Jesus walks in the temple courts, the chief priests, the teachers of the law, and the elders come to him. They represent the recognized authority—the leadership of the temple and its practices—and they have come to challenge Jesus. He has driven the money changers and sellers of merchandise out of the temple courts. He has taught the people, speaking with a level of wisdom and authority that astounds those who hear him. Mark makes it clear that these leaders are afraid. They are afraid of Jesus because the people gathered in the temple are so amazed at his teaching, and they are afraid of angering the people if they say something that implies John the Baptist was not a prophet from God. Who is in charge here? Who is encroaching on whose territory? If we have been following Mark carefully in our Lenten reading, we will realize that in this passage for today Mark is messing with our minds.

The temple establishment is utterly corrupt during this era in Jerusalem. There is greed, hypocrisy, infighting, and constant tension. As we read the various Gospel accounts of the arrest and trial of Jesus before the Jewish Sanhedrin (the ruling council of the temple at the time), we see evidence that there is even conflict over who is the legitimate high priest. In Mark, when Jesus enters the temple, everything changes. What once was the location and representation of the presence of God in the midst of the people of Israel for the sake of the world is now completely undone. It has lost all legitimacy. The final blow is the utter and bitter refusal of religious leadership to recognize who Jesus is. Into the temple courts has come the One who is now the perfect embodiment of God, the representation of all that the people of God were intended to be.

It is no wonder the Jewish leaders are terrified. It is obvious to them that Jesus is a mortal threat to their authority. They know, without any hesitation, that the only way to protect their authority is to do away with Jesus, to kill him, to see that this pretender is destroyed. This is their religious duty. So they begin to plot their way into oblivion. Their presumed authority is up against the ultimate sovereignty of the incarnate Son of God. "Crucify him!" they will later shout, thinking that, if they end his life, they can preserve their place, their authority.

If the Lenten journey is teaching us anything, it might be best summed up thus: the arrogance of sin is to believe that, if we can just do away with all competitors to our own authority, our own sovereignty, then we can be free. But the One who took upon himself the form of a servant, who became "obedient to death—even death on a cross!" knows best that our greatest freedom is found in our submission to him (Philippians 2:7, 8).

Maybe it is time to ask ourselves: who is in charge here?

—JCM

REFLECTION & PRACTICE

01 The religious leaders understand themselves to be guardians of their sacred tradition. However, their hardness of heart prevents them

from perceiving God's movement in the very tradition they seek to protect. They fall prey to the sin of gatekeeping and power hoarding.

- We too want to protect the tradition(s) handed down to us. How do we guard against hardness of heart that might prevent us from seeing new things that God might be doing among us?
- Where have you seen the sin of gatekeeping and power hoarding at work in the church? In your own heart and life? What would it look like to repent and go a new way?

02 The temple is a sacred place. It is the physical embodiment of the intersection of the heavenly and earthly realms. It is intended to be a sign of the future age in which heaven and earth become one and God dwells with God's people forever. But, over time, the sign was mistaken for the destination. The gift became an idol and an instrument of power and control.

- What signs might we mistake for the destination? What things might the church value to an idolatrous degree, so much so that they distract us from the end goal—namely, God's reign expressed through us?
- How might we be guilty of taking the gifts of God and misshaping them into instruments of power and control?

03 The narrative of Western culture equates freedom with self-sovereignty with no remainder.

- What falsehoods undergird that narrative?
- How might true freedom be found in surrender?
- How might surrender actually enable us to be more fully human?

PRAYER

Lord, we are grateful for tradition that has been passed down to us. We confess that, at times, we have made an idol of the gifts you have given to us instead of stewarding them for the sake of the world. Forgive us for fixing our eyes on anything but you. May our hearts be sensitive to your Spirit's whispers of conviction and correction, that we may worship and serve you faithfully.

WEDNESDAY OF HOLY WEEK

AM *Psalm: 55*

PM *Psalm: 74*

Lamentations 2:1–9

Mark 12:1–11

2 Corinthians 1:23–2:11

The Parable of the Vineyard is the most straightforward of the parables of Jesus. Other parables were often subtle in their meaning, forcing hearers to wrestle with the story, talk about it, and debate its application. In this case the point of the story is stunningly clear.

There is a remarkable parallel between this parable and the Song of the Vineyard in Isaiah 5:1–7. The use of a vineyard metaphor in reference to Israel is not at all unusual. The hearers of the Parable of the Vineyard would understand the reference without any need for explanation. The parable is a historical review of the relationship the people, especially the leaders of Israel, have had with the God of Israel. Time and again God has reached out to Israel in mercy and grace, forming them for relationship with God and anticipating their participation in the mission of God. Repeatedly Israel has failed to keep the covenant of love God created with them. They have abused the prophets sent to call them back to the covenant. The Song of the Vineyard in Isaiah 5 gives voice to the anguish of God that the vineyard has produced only bad fruit, worth nothing, and in danger of abandonment.

In Jesus's parable, the vineyard is fruitful. Its owner is pleased with the productivity of the vineyard and sends his representative to collect his portion of the fruit. But in Jesus's telling of the parable, a shift has occurred. The emphasis is now on the tenants, the stewards of the vineyard. Their responsibility has been to steward this resource on behalf of the owner. Once trusted colleagues, they have become betrayers. They have rejected the rights of the owner and claimed priority for themselves. An escalating tension leads at last to the owner sending his son, trusting that the stewards, once they see the son, will relent, restore the vineyard to its rightful owner, and return to their proper place as stewards. And they kill the son! But the owner is still the owner, the vineyard is still capable of producing fruit, and the tenants are doomed.

The chief priests, the teachers of the law, and the elders have not missed the point of the parable. They know it is directed at them, and they are furious. Their fiercely protected status is more tenuous than they know, but they can read the writing on the wall, and they fear the people, knowing that if they arrest Jesus they could well provoke a riot.

How is it that, given their own history—the repeated experiences of exile, their domination by the Roman Empire, and the four hundred years since the last prophetic communication—they do not allow themselves to see God when God shows up? Sin obscures our vision. Sin in which we *persist* blinds us entirely. And, for those in power, the light that shines into that darkness must be eliminated.

In the Gospel of Mark, the developing revelation of the identity of Jesus as Son of God marches relentlessly on. May our Lenten journey provide unresisted light, and may we relinquish our self-obsessed possessiveness to the rightful Owner.

—JCM

REFLECTION & PRACTICE

01 This is a hard parable, but do not miss the first verse. The vineyard owner is deeply invested in the health of the vine. The owner's provision, care, and protection reveal a commitment to the vine's flourishing. This is God's commitment to Israel, and to those of us who have been grafted in.

- How did God demonstrate divine provision, care, and protection to Israel?
- How has God demonstrated the same in your life?
- What does this reveal about God's desire for creation?

02 Those who were entrusted with the task of stewarding the vine, God's precious people, were unfaithful to their task. They usurped power and authority and acted violently toward those who attempted to hold them to account.

- Have you witnessed (or participated in) the abuse of power and lack of accountability in the church? What were the consequences?
- While this is primarily an indictment on the leaders of God's people, all followers of Jesus are stewards of and participants in God's mission of redemption. In what ways might we abandon our given role as stewards and usurp the power, authority, and rule of God?

03 In spite of the stewards' unfaithfulness, the vineyard is fruitful. God is on the move, and God's mission will not be thwarted by human rebellion. Rather, God will invite others to join the work of the harvest.

- How might the reminder that the harvest is in fact ripe be both a word of comfort and correction?
- How might a healthy embrace of our role as stewards and co-laborers with God protect us from the idolatry of the religious leaders addressed in this parable?

PRAYER

Lord, your love for us pulses through this text even as you call our sin to account. You desire that we flourish and grow, for our sake and the sake of the world. We confess that we have not always been faithful in our role as stewards of your gifts but have instead hoarded and abused them for our own benefit. Forgive us when we assume authority and control that are yours alone. Give us the grace of being put in our proper place, for your glory and our good.

MAUNDY
THURSDAY

AM *Psalm: 102*

PM *Psalms: 142, 143*

Lamentations 2:10–18

Mark 14:12–25

1 Corinthians 10:14–17; 11:27–32

It is Maundy Thursday of Holy Week. "Maundy," from the Latin word for "commandment," is in recognition of the commandment Jesus gave to his disciples in that final celebration of Passover: "My command is this: Love each other as I have loved you" (John 15:12). The incongruity of that setting is stark. The Passover celebration was a looking back, a remembrance of what God did in delivering Israel from their slavery in Egypt. It was, and still is, the most central religious observance in Judaism. But Jesus is reshaping the entire narrative. As he shares the broken bread and poured-out wine, he gives them new meaning. He is not merely looking back to the death of the firstborn of Egypt that precipitated Israel's deliverance from slavery. He is also looking ahead to his own death on the cross as the basis of their deliverance from the power of sin and death. This is to inaugurate a new way of being in the world. Everything is being turned on its head!

In observing Passover with his disciples Jesus seeks to prepare the Twelve for all that is about to happen to him. It is obvious that they are still confused about what he is saying, and still confident in their ability to manage whatever is rushing toward them. It is also obvious that Jesus is continuing to reach out in love to everyone in the room—including his betrayer, Judas. Judas was not excluded from the invitation to participate in the Passover. What grace!

In the act of leading the disciples through the Passover meal, Jesus foreshadows his own death. "This is my body," he says of the bread (Mark 14:22). "This is my blood of the covenant," he says of the wine. In a stunning reinterpretation of the meaning of those essential elements in the traditional Passover meal, Jesus brings the Old Testament sacrificial system to a conclusion. All that is signified in the celebration of Passover for the Jewish people has now come to fulfillment in the death of Jesus. It is important to note that the lamb, sacrificed in preparation for being eaten at the Passover meal, is never referenced in the accounts of this Passover celebration. Jesus, the Lamb of God, has initiated the new covenant. This new covenant is not limited to the few, the people of Israel. It is extended to the many. All of humanity is now invited in the covenant established through the blood of the Lamb.

The Twelve—including Judas and whoever else is part of that pivotal evening—are not yet there. The desperate need for this new covenant is demonstrated in that the betrayer carries out his dastardly deed, and all remaining of the Twelve desert Jesus at the arrest or the trial and go into hiding.

However, the new covenant defeats the powers of sin and death. The new kingdom is established. The death Jesus dies redeems all of those who so miserably fail that fateful evening. And for all of humanity—for anyone, anywhere, at any time who responds to his hand outstretched in love—there is redemption. Oh, what love.

—JCM

REFLECTION & PRACTICE

01 The command of Passover is to remember. Remember what God did for the people of God. Remember God's deliverance and provision. Jesus's identification with the bread and wine of the feast is not a break from the story of God or an appropriation of a sacred tradition. It is the culmination of the story—God's deliverance from the ultimate enemy and God's provision of a Deliverer. Remember. Pause and remember the deliverance of the people of Israel from Egypt. Remember the disciples gathered around the table. Remember the taste of the bread and wine on your own tongue. From what has God delivered you? How have you borne witness to God's provision?

02 It is easy to forget Judas's presence at the table. It would be more comfortable for us if Jesus had already dismissed him to do the work at hand. But no, Jesus intentionally includes the betrayer at the table of fellowship.

- How does this unsettling inclusion of the enemy impact how we hear the command of this night: "Love one another as I have loved you?"
- How might we practice an open table? Who needs to be invited? Who needs to be asked to stay and eat?

03 The deliverance initiated by the new covenant is not from a specific manifestation of evil, like Pharaoh or Caesar, but deliverance from the powers of sin and death. The long-awaited kingdom will be inaugurated when Jesus is glorified on the cross and ultimately raised to new creation life. The new covenant makes clear that we are free. Not slaves, but adopted children and co-heirs with Christ. Do we live as those freed from sin and death? How might our daily lives testify to the deliverance wrought by Jesus's life, death, and resurrection?

PRAYER

Lord, thank you for withholding nothing from us but instead giving yourself entirely to deliver us from the powers of sin and death. You have welcomed us to the table of salvation, sin-sick and changeable though we are. We confess our faithlessness and our persistent blindness. Open our eyes to the broken chains that lie at our feet, and give us the courage by your Spirit to walk forward into the freedom of new creation life. May we use our freedom to love as we have been loved.

GOOD FRIDAY

AM *Psalms: 22, 95*

PM *Psalms: 40, 54*

Lamentations 3:1–9, 19–33

AM *Gospel Reading: John 13:36–38*

PM *Gospel Reading: John 19:38–42*

1 Peter 1:10–20

Good Friday? What on earth could give anyone the idea that this day in the life of Jesus could be termed, in any conceivable way, *good?* On this day of Holy Week, we recall a narrative that is hard to fathom. Jesus is betrayed by one of his own, is later denied by one of his closest companions, and is deserted by all but a few: John and many of the women followers. He is arrested and shuffled back and forth between Jewish religious leaders and Roman officials. He is tortured, condemned to die, and crucified.

Jeremiah gives voice to the anguish Jesus must have felt: "He has walled me in so I cannot escape; he has weighed me down with chains. Even when I call out or cry for help, he shuts out my prayer" (Lamentations 3:7–8). In reading Psalm 22, we hear the cry of Jesus from the cross:

"My God, my God, why have you forsaken me?" (v. 1). The echoes of the scoffers who threw their insults at Jesus are seen in verses 7 and 8. Jesus was obviously very familiar with these words. In his agony and despair, the cry of his heart came right out of the anguished words of that psalm.

Joseph of Arimathea and Nicodemus take a dangerous risk in asking permission to take the body of Jesus down from the cross and prepare it for burial. Pressed for time, and now identified with the followers of Jesus by this very act, they move quickly to wrap the body in spices and strips of linen. What must be their conversation? How do you bring closure to what you hoped would be the advent of Israel's long-awaited Messiah? The shattered body, the setting sun, the deepening darkness, the quiet desperation: do these seem to validate the wisdom of their choice to remain secret disciples? Death is so final! "'My splendor is gone and all that I had hoped from the LORD.' I remember my affliction and my wandering, the bitterness and the gall" (Lamentations 3:18–19).

The intent of Good Friday is remembrance. This is a day of the year when we should not rush past the details, the realization of the cost of our redemption. This day, of all days, should humble us. Spend time in quiet meditation. Ponder the implication that, apart from the suffering death of Jesus on our behalf, we would have no hope. The good was not in the agony and suffering death. The good was what the agony and suffering and death accomplished for all. And in that suffering was the pattern for all that his kingdom represents. As Peter wrote, "For you know that it was not with perishable things such as silver or gold that you were redeemed from the empty way of life handed down to you from your ancestors, but with the precious blood of Christ, a lamb without blemish or defect" (1 Peter 1:18–19). This may not be the good we thought we wanted. But it is indeed the good we desperately need, and it is the good we get. Thanks be to God!

—JCM

REFLECTION & PRACTICE

01 The Gospel writers do not whitewash the crucifixion or Jesus's experience of it. He suffers physically. He watches the majority of his beloved friends—in whom he has invested so much the past three years—abandon him without so much as a backward glance. Overcome by sorrow and loss, Jesus feels forsaken by the Father. The

ancient church father Gregory of Nazianzus said of Christ's incarnation, "What has not been assumed has not been healed." How does Jesus's suffering open up the possibility of our healing from the pain of loss, betrayal, and feeling abandoned by God?

02 We cannot pretend not to know the ending of this story. We know the resurrection is coming. However, we cannot skip over death to arrive at the empty tomb unscathed. We must enter the tomb with Christ, watch the stone extinguish the last sliver of light, and wait with only trust to sustain us. Pause in the tomb with Christ. Allow yourself to feel the weight of the powers of sin and death and reflect on the havoc these powers have wreaked in and around you. Confess your complicity as well as your powerlessness to mend what is broken.

03 We remember Good Friday year after year. Why? The outcome does not change. Judas does not have a change of heart. Jesus does not decide to assemble his followers and fight back. Yet we return to the same story again and again. The same betrayal, the same refusal to answer violence with violence, the same submission unto death. How does repeated immersion and participation in the story of God reform us? How might this discipline elicit deeper trust and faithfulness?

PRAYER

Lord, once again we find ourselves face to face with a sealed tomb. The blood on the cross is not yet dry. How could our beloved be in the grave? You went willingly, like a lamb before slaughter, for us and for our salvation. We cannot raise our fists in anger at those who struck you, for we are complicit. We too have chosen violence over forgiveness, self over submission. We too have gone our own way. Yet we are also the victims of the sins of others. Broken, we fall at your nail-pierced feet and plead for forgiveness and healing. How could we have known the cost? We are overwhelmed by the goodness of your love.

HOLY SATURDAY

AM *Psalms: 95, 88*

PM *Psalm: 27*

Lamentations 3:37–58

AM *Epistle Reading: Hebrews 4:1–16*

PM *Epistle Reading: Romans 8:1–11*

There is hardly anyplace more silent than a graveyard. Other than family members, people seldom visit them once they have left a service of committal. Pastors are the ones who most frequently find themselves ministering to a family, leading a funeral service, and presiding over the final moments before a body is laid in a grave or ashes placed in a columbarium. Conversations among friends and family are—for hours, sometimes days—held in hushed tones. Sometimes unanswerable questions come. *Why? How did this happen? What are we going to do?*

It is Holy Saturday. Sometimes we call it Silent or Black Saturday. This is the day on which we get glimpses of the struggles that followed the burial of Jesus. His followers were crushed. Some wrestled with deep grief and regret. Others were simply confused beyond their understanding. And they questioned. *Why did this happen? What are we going to do?*

On this silent Saturday, on the eve of Easter, we do well to ponder and think deeply. But we must also acknowledge that it is hard to grieve deeply over the crucifixion when we live our lives in the light of the resurrection rather than in the shadow of the cross. We are at a distinct advantage over the first followers of Jesus for that reason alone. But our awareness that Easter is just over the horizon should not distract us from pondering the significance of the crucifixion.

Jeremiah, grieving over the destruction of Jerusalem and the scattering of the people of Israel in exile, cried out, "Why should the living complain when punished for their sins? Let us examine our ways and test them, and let us return to the LORD" (Lamentations 3:39–40). Like Israel, we desperately need to return to God, but one of the realities we face is that, on our own, there is no way that we can. The apostle Paul put the issue in the clearest terms: "Sin entered the world through one man, and death through sin, and in this way death came to all people, because all sinned" (Romans 5:12). Our sin so destroyed our ability to turn toward God that none of us, without exception, could ever do enough to make our way to God or to overcome death. That is the point of the Lenten journey. We know that, on our own, we are powerless, bound in sin, doomed to death. But "God made him who had no sin to be sin for us, so that in him we might become the righteousness of God" (2 Corinthians 5:21). "All this is from God, who reconciled us to himself through Christ and gave us the ministry of reconciliation" (2 Corinthians 5:18).

On this silent, black Saturday, we must remind ourselves that Jesus spent that day in the tomb because our sins put him there. It was for us that he died. But in his death, all things have been reconciled to God. New creation has begun. Life is about to break out all over the world. You will want to sing! But not yet. Take just a little more time. Grieve over the sin. It's not Sunday yet.

—JCM

REFLECTION & PRACTICE

01 The day following Jesus's crucifixion was the Sabbath. The disciples, overcome by fear, sorrow, and confusion had minimal resources accessible to them to manage that experience. They could not go for a long walk to think. They could not busy themselves in the garden in

an attempt to occupy their minds. No fishing to distract the senses. Only stillness. Waiting for what, they knew not.

- What habits or patterns do we employ to avoid the painful stillness and the seemingly interminable wait for God to act?
- On this Holy Saturday, challenge yourself to set aside a habit or activity that you might typically use as a distraction. Wait in the stillness without expectation.

02 Psalm 88, one of today's morning psalms, is unique. Most psalms, particularly lament psalms, end with a return to praise, a holy turnaround from sorrow to trust. Psalm 88 does not. It ends with questions, fear, and doubt.

- In many ways, our lives move in and out of the difficult space of Holy Saturday. Doubt plagues. Pain persists. There is no quick turnaround to deliverance. When have you found yourself in the painful space of Holy Saturday? How did God meet with you there?
- How might an honest wrestling with the Holy Saturday experience of others enable us to practice holy empathy?

03 When we have journeyed with Jesus through the Gospels, when we have followed him to the cross, and when we have sat next to the silent tomb—then and only then are we ready to rise with him and sing "Alleluia!" How has this Lenten journey prepared your heart to celebrate Easter with joy and gratitude?

PRAYER

Lord, like the disciples long ago, we sit in silence on this difficult day. You are in the tomb. Though we know the resurrection awaits us tomorrow, we deeply resonate with the tension of this day. We have known hurts unresolved and sorrow unabated. We are on a first-name basis with doubt, fear, confusion, and uncertainty. Yet we know you are the God of resurrection. And so, in the silence, we do not lose heart. In the stillness, we do not surrender to fear. We trust you. We wait for you.

EASTER SUNDAY

AM *Psalms: 148, 149, 150*

AM *Old Testament Reading: Exodus 12:1-14*

AM *Gospel Reading: John 1:1-18*

PM *Psalms: 113, 114, or 118*

PM *Old Testament Reading: Isaiah 51:9-11*

PM *Gospel Reading: Luke 24:13-35 or John 20:19-23*

It is Easter Sunday, and the news is good! In contrast to the somber notes of Maundy Thursday, the horror of Good Friday, and the stunned silence of a painful Sabbath, there suddenly rings a note of ferocious hope! From the lips of women—the least likely candidates, in that culture at that time, to be entrusted with communicating important news—comes a confusing, stunning assertion that Jesus is alive! What follows is little less than chaos: men running toward the gravesite, angels appearing in an empty tomb, two people encountering the risen Lord on their way home, and fearful disciples huddled behind locked doors.

When you are enduring the pain of searing loss, it is difficult to tolerate joy. People who bring news of stunning reversal, who insist that you believe the inconceivable, can grate on already frayed nerves. Hope once ignited, then extinguished, by the cruelty of crucifixion dares not hope again. But that is the very nature of hope! It will not stay dead! That is the assertion of Isaiah to a people suffering exile, rejection, despair, deprivation, and a loss of hope for redemption. "Awake, awake, arm of the LORD, clothe yourself with strength! Awake, as in days gone by, as in generations of old. . . . Was it not you who dried up the sea, the waters of the great deep, who made a road in the depths of the sea so that the redeemed might cross over? Those the LORD has rescued will return. They will enter Zion with singing; everlasting joy will crown their heads. Gladness and joy will overtake them, and sorrow and sighing will flee away" (Isaiah 51:9a, 10–11).

Given our advantage of two thousand years of celebrations, we can easily overlook the confusion, the uncertainty, and the chaos of that first Easter. No one seemed to remember, at first, that Jesus had told them this would happen. It was a matter of repeated insistence that they should be prepared for this very occurrence, yet they were still stunned as the events unfolded. But God has always acted beyond our capacity to comprehend what grace will do. After this journey through the season of Lent, allow the good news of Easter to capture your imagination with wonder. Sing Psalm 150 with the psalmist:

Praise the LORD.
Praise God in his sanctuary;
praise him in his mighty heavens.
Praise him for his acts of power;
praise him for his surpassing greatness.
Praise him for with the sounding of the trumpet,
praise him with the harp and lyre,
praise him with timbrel and dancing,
praise him with the strings and pipe,
praise him with the clash of cymbals,
praise him with resounding cymbals.
Let everything that has breath praise the LORD.
Praise the LORD.

—JCM

REFLECTION & PRACTICE

01 "Hope ignited, then extinguished, dares not hope again." We fear we will be made fools by hope. Our hearts harden and minds close to protect us from the risk of hoping yet again.

- In what ways have our hearts been hardened in self-protection against disappointment and unrealized hopes?
- How does this resistance to hope, unconscious or not, shape our relationship with God and others?

02 Hope is indefatigable. It continues to spring forth even in dry, dusty soil. This hope is the fruit of resurrection power at work in creation and in us. It persists against all odds.

- Where have you witnessed hope springing forth in unexpected places and times? How did this experience impact you?
- What might it look like to be a people marked by eternal hope? How would this change our response to circumstances and people that seem beyond the reach of hope?

03 The resurrection of Jesus is the quintessential example of God acting far beyond what our imaginations could conjure or our hearts hope for.

- In light of the shocking act of God in raising Jesus from the dead, how might we surrender our imaginations to God and allow God to dream God-size dreams in us?
- How might our churches be transformed if we allowed our corporate imagination to be formed by the power of the resurrection? How might we steward our resources differently? Engage with vital issues in our community differently?

PRAYER

Heavenly Father, today we celebrate once again the resurrection of your Son, Jesus, by the power of the Spirit. We confess that, like the disciples who struggled to believe that you could overcome death, we struggle to believe that the power of the resurrection is still at work in us and in creation. Bearing the wounds of broken promises and empty hopes, we choose self-protection over hope, self-reliance over trust. Heal us, that we might

live freely in the hope you offer. Unleash your resurrection power in us,
that we might become your resurrection people for the sake of the world.

ABOUT THE AUTHORS

DR. JESSE C MIDDENDORF is executive director of the Center for Pastoral Leadership at Nazarene Theological Seminary. He served for twenty-eight years as a pastor in the Church of the Nazarene, five years as a district superintendent, and twelve years as a general superintendent, retiring in 2013. He and his wife, Susan, have been married for more than fifty-five years and have three children and six grandchildren.

REV. STEPHANIE DYRNESS LOBDELL, MDiv, is a pastor and writer. She served as co-lead pastor with her husband, Tommy, for ten years in the Church of the Nazarene and is now the campus pastor at Mount Vernon Nazarene University in Ohio. Stephanie and Tommy have two children, Josephine and Jack.